Malebranche

The Seminars of Alain Badiou

The Seminars of Alain Badiou

Kenneth Reinhard, General Editor

Alain Badiou is widely considered to be one of the most important Continental philosophers of our time. Badiou has developed much of his thinking in his annual seminars, which he delivered in Paris from the late 1970s to 2017. These seminars include discussions that inform his major books, including *Being and Event*, *Logics of Worlds*, and *The Immanence of Truths*, as well as presentations of many ideas and topics that are not part of his published work. Some volumes of the seminar investigate individual thinkers and writers such as Parmenides, Plato, Nietzsche, Heidegger, Beckett, and Mallarmé. Others examine concepts such as infinity, truth, the subject, the present, evil, love, and the nature of change. These seminars constitute an essential part of Badiou's thinking, one that remains largely unknown to the non-Francophone world. Their translation is a major event for philosophers and other scholars and students in the humanities and social sciences and for the artists, writers, political theorists, and engaged intellectuals for whom Badiou's work has rapidly become a generative and inspiring resource.

For a complete list of seminars, see page 195.

Malebranche

Theological Figure, Being 2

Alain Badiou

Translated by
Jason E. Smith with Susan Spitzer

Introduction by Jason E. Smith

Columbia University Press
New York

Columbia University Press
Publishers Since 1893
New York Chichester, West Sussex
cup.columbia.edu

First published in French as *Le Séminaire—Malebranche: L'Être 2—
Figure théologique (1986)*
© 2013 Librairie Arthème Fayard

Library of Congress Cataloging-in-Publication Data
Names: Badiou, Alain, author.
Title: Malebranche, theological figure, being 2 / Alain Badiou ; translated
by Jason E. Smith ; introduction by Kenneth Reinhard.
Other titles: Malebranche, figure theologique, 1986. English
Description: New York : Columbia University Press, 2018. | Includes
bibliographical references and index.
Identifiers: LCCN 2018030133 (print) | LCCN 2018051116 (e-book) |
ISBN 9780231548533 (e-book) | ISBN 9780231174787 (cloth : alk. paper)
Subjects: LCSH: Malebranche, Nicolas, 1638-1715. | Malebranche, Nicolas,
1638-1715. Traite de la nature et de la grace.
Classification: LCC B1897 (ebook) | LCC B1897 .B3413 2018 (print) |
DDC 194—dc23
LC record available at https://lccn.loc.gov/2018030133

Columbia University Press books are printed on permanent
and durable acid-free paper.
Printed in the United States of America

Cover design: Julia Kushnirsky

Contents

Editors' Introduction to the English Edition of the Seminars of Alain Badiou vii

Author's General Preface to the English Edition of the Seminars of Alain Badiou xi

Introduction to the Seminar on Malebranche: Malebranche's "Political Ontology"

(Jason E. Smith) xxi

About the 1986 Seminar on Malebranche xxxv

Session 1   1

Session 2   29

Session 3   53

Session 4   81

Session 5   101

Session 6   129

Session 7   155

Notes   177

Index   183

Editors' Introduction to the English Edition of the Seminars of Alain Badiou

KENNETH REINHARD, SUSAN SPITZER, AND JASON E. SMITH

With the publication in English of Alain Badiou's seminar, we believe that a new phase of his reception in the Anglophone world will open up, one that bridges the often formidable gap between the two main forms in which his published work has so far appeared. On the one hand, there is the tetralogy of his difficult and lengthy major works of systematic philosophy, beginning with a sort of prelude, *Theory of the Subject*, and continuing with the three parts of *Being and Event*, *Logics of Worlds*, and the forthcoming *Immanence of Truths*. On the other hand, there are his numerous shorter and occasional pieces on topics such as ethics, contemporary politics, film, literature, and art. Badiou's "big books" are often built on rather daunting mathematical ideas and formulations: *Being and Event* relies primarily on set theory and the innovations introduced by Paul Cohen; *Logics of Worlds* adds category, topos, and sheaf theory; and *The Immanence of Truths* expands into the mathematics of large cardinals. Each of these great works is written in its own distinctive, and often rather dense, style: *Theory of the Subject* echoes the dramatic tone and form of a Lacanian seminar; *Being and Event* presents a fundamental ontology in the form of a series of Cartesian "meditations"; *Logics of Worlds* is organized in formal theories and "Greater Logics," and expressed in richly developed concrete examples, phenomenological descriptions, and scholia; and for reading the *Immanence of Truths*, Badiou suggests two distinct paths: one short and "absolutely necessary," the other long and "more elaborate or illustrative, more free-ranging." Because of the difficulty of these longer books, and their highly compact formulations, Badiou's shorter writings—such as the books on ethics and Saint Paul—often serve as a reader's first point of entry into his ideas. But this less steep path of induction brings its own problems, insofar as these more topical and occasional works often take for granted their relationship to the fundamental architecture of Badiou's thinking and thus may appear to have a greater (or smaller) role in it than they actually do. Hence the publication of Badiou's seminar from 1983 through (at least) 2012 makes available a middle path, one in which the major lines of Badiou's thinking—as well as its many extraordinary detours—are displayed with the remarkable clarity and the generous explications and exemplifications that always characterize his oral presentations.[1] It is extraordinarily exciting to see the genesis of Badiou's ideas in the experimental and performative context of his seminar, and there is a great deal in the seminars that doesn't appear at all in his existing published writings.

The first volume of the seminar to be published in English, on Lacan, constitutes part of a four-year sequence on "anti-philosophy" which also includes volumes on Nietzsche, Wittgenstein, and Saint Paul. The second volume, on Malebranche, is part of a similar cluster on being, which also involves years dedicated to Parmenides and Heidegger. And the later volumes, beginning in 1996, gather material from multiple years of the seminar, as in the case of *Axiomatic Theory of the Subject* (which is based on the sessions from the years 1996–97 and 1997–98), and *Images of the Present Time* (which was delivered in sessions over three years, from 2001 to 2004).

Isabelle Vodoz and Véronique Pineau are establishing the French text of the seminar on the basis of audio recordings and notes, with the intention of remaining as close as possible to Badiou's delivery while eliminating unnecessary repetitions and other minor artifacts. In reviewing and approving the texts of the seminar (sometimes as long as thirty years after having delivered them), Badiou decided not to revise or reformulate them, but to let them speak for themselves, without the benefit of self-critical hindsight. Given this decision, it is remarkable to see how consistent his thinking has been over the years. Moreover, each volume of the seminar includes a preface by Badiou that offers an extremely valuable account of the political and intellectual context of the seminar, as well as a sort of retrospective reflection on the process of his thought's emergence. In our translations of the seminar into English, we have tried to preserve the oral quality of the French edition in order to give the reader the impression of listening to the original recordings. We hope that the publication of Badiou's seminar will allow more readers to encounter the full scope of his ideas, and will allow those readers who are already familiar with his work to discover a new sense of its depths, its range, and its implications—perhaps almost as if reading Badiou for the first time.

The Seminars of Alain Badiou (1983–2016): General Preface

ALAIN BADIOU

The Seminars in English

It is a great pleasure for me to write this preface to the English-language edition of the entire collection of thirty years of my seminars. The information below is intended simply to shed some light on what these thirty years of public speaking have meant, to me and my various audiences, and why there may be some interest, or even pleasure, to be found in reading the seminars.

I. A Few Historical Reference Points

The word "seminar" should, in principle, refer to collective work around a particular problem. Instead, where these seminars are concerned, it refers to my own individual, albeit public, work on many different problems, all of which were nonetheless united by a philosophical apparatus explicitly claiming to be systematic.

Admittedly, the word "seminar" was already used in the latter sense with reference to Lacan's famous seminar, which, for me and many other people, has raised the bar very high when it comes to this sort of thing.

That a large part of my teaching took the form of such a seminar—whose ongoing publication in French, and now in English and

Spanish, will show that it remained virtually free from any institutional authority—was originally due to pure chance.

At the beginning of the academic year 1966–67, while I was the senior class teacher at the boys' high school in Reims, I was appointed lecturer in an establishment that had just been created and that testified to the rapid expansion of higher education in the supremely Gaullist France of those years: the Collège universitaire de Reims, affiliated with the University of Nancy. Initially, only so-called propaedeutic [i.e., college preparatory] teaching was to be provided there (at the time, there was a first year of studies with that name, validated by a final exam that, if successfully passed, allowed students to begin their first year of university). So I was asked to teach the philosophy option in this preparatory year. But all of a sudden, thanks to one of those nasty betrayals so typical of academic life, the University of Nancy announced that, for the time being, it couldn't relinquish its philosophical powers to Reims and that there wouldn't be any philosophy option for the preparatory program to which my position was attached.

So there I was, a teacher of a nonexistent discipline. Given these circumstances, what else was there to do but hold an open seminar? And that's what I did for two years (1966–67 and 1967–68), before—I have to brag a bit here—an increasingly large audience and, what was even more flattering to me, one that was there out of pure interest since there was no final exam to reward their faithful attendance.

If I'd had the energy to look for my notes from that time long ago (when no one had either the idea or the means to bring in one of those big, clunky tape recorders to record my improvisations) and to revise those notes and turn them into a written text, I could have proudly begun this edition of the seminars with the one from 1966–67—fifty years of free speech!—, the year devoted to Schopenhauer, and then continued with the 1967–68 seminar, when my syllabus was focused on Mallarmé, Rimbaud, and Lautréamont, in that order. The *Chants de Maldoror*, however, which I had intended to begin dealing with in early May, was sacrificed on the altar of the mass movement.

And then, as a result of that May upheaval, which was to drastically change my life and my thinking about many issues other than academic appointments, I was appointed (since those appointments continued to be made nonetheless) Assistant Professor at the Experimental University of Vincennes, which soon became Paris 8.

The context in which I began teaching courses there was so feverish and politically so intense, the actions afoot there so radical, that the government decided that the philosophy degrees granted by Paris 8 would have no national accreditation! So there I was again, forced to give an open seminar since there was no state validation of our teaching efforts, despite the fact that they were highly innovative, to say the least.

This marginalization lasted for years. So—if, once again, the documentation really allowed for it—I could give an account of the free and open seminars of the 1970s, which, when all the exciting, frenetic collective action going on at the time allowed them to take place, were devoted in particular to the Hegelian dialectic, to Mallarmé again, to my beloved Plato, and to Lacan, always before audiences that were there out of pure interest alone, since there was no exam and therefore no academic credit to validate their attendance.

Actually, a synthetic account of that period does exist: my book *Theory of the Subject*, published by Seuil in 1982 under the editorship of François Wahl (English translation published by Continuum, 2009). It provides an admittedly very freely rewritten account of the seminars that were held between January 1975 and June 1979.

Beginning in those years, as a result of the so-called political normalization, things calmed down in the universities, even in the one in Vincennes, which had incidentally been moved to Saint-Denis. In the early 1980s, the government authorities decided that we of the glorious Department of Philosophy—where you could hear lectures by Michel Foucault, Michel Serres, François Châtelet, Gilles Deleuze, Jean-François Lyotard, and Jacques Rancière—deserved to have the national accreditation we'd lost gradually restored. It was from that time on, too, that the seminars began to be systematically recorded by several different attendees. Little wonder, then, that I decided to publish all of the seminars between 1983 and the present: for these thirty-odd years, abundant, continuous documentation exists.

Not that the locations, the institutions, and the frequency didn't change. Indeed, starting in 1987 the seminar moved to the Collège international de philosophie, which owed its creation in large part to the determined efforts of everyone in "living [i.e. non-traditional] philosophy" who felt put down and badmouthed by the University, Lyotard and Derrida being the two most emblematic names at the time. In that setting, I rediscovered the innocence of teaching without exams or validation: the seminar was now officially open and free of charge to everyone (for the reasons I mentioned above, it had actually always been so). It was held in the locales that the Collège secured or bargained hard to secure for its activities: the old École polytechnique on the rue Descartes, the École normale supérieure on the boulevard Jourdan, an industrial institution on the rue de Varenne, the Institut catholique on the rue d'Assas, and the main auditorium of the University of Paris 7 at Jussieu.

In 1998, when my seminar had been held under the auspices of the Collège international de philosophie for ten years, a crisis of sorts erupted: one faction of the Collège's administration viewed with suspicion both the form and the content of what I was doing. As far as the form was concerned, my status in the Collège was an exceptional one since, although I'd initially been properly inducted into it under Philippe Lacoue-Labarthe's presidency, I had never been officially re-elected as a member of the Collège. The content was viewed with suspicion because in those times dominated by the antitotalitarian ideology of human rights, rumors were going around that my teaching was "fascist." As I was unwilling to put up with such an atmosphere, I broke off my seminar midyear, thereby causing a lot of confusion.

I set it up the following fall at the École normale supérieure, where I'd been appointed professor. It remained there for fifteen years, which is pretty good, after all.

But this seminar was fated to always end up antagonizing institutions. I had to use the largest lecture halls at the ENS due to the sizeable audiences the seminar attracted, but at the start of the 2014 school year there was a dark plot afoot to deny me all access to those rooms and recommend that I accommodate around 250 people in a room that held only 80! After driving Lacan out, the prestigious ENS drove me out too! But, after all, I told myself, to suffer the same fate as Lacan was in its own way a glorious destiny. What happened to me next, however, can literally be called a "coup de théâtre," a dramatic turn of events. My friend Marie-José Malis, the outstanding theater artist and great renovator of the art of directing, was appointed artistic director of the Théâtre de la Commune in the Paris suburb of Aubervilliers. She offered to let me hold my seminar there, and I enthusiastically accepted. For two and a half years, in the heart of a working-class suburb, I stood on the stage before a full house and interspersed my final seminars, which were connected with the writing of my last "big" book, L'Immanence des vérités, with actual theatrical presentations. I was generously assisted in this by Didier Galas, who created the role of Ahmed in my four-play cycle, written in the 1980s and 1990s for the artistic and stage director Christian Schiaretti: Ahmed the Subtle, Ahmed Gets Angry, Ahmed the Philosopher, and The Pumpkins. On January 16, 2017, my Final Seminar took place in the Théâtre de la Commune in Aubervilliers, where pure philosophy, congratulatory messages, anecdotes, and theatrical productions all combined to celebrate the seminar's long history for one last time.

I'd always wanted the seminar to be for people who worked. That's why, for a very long time, it took place between 8 and 10 PM, on Tuesdays for a few years, on Wednesdays for probably twenty years, if not more, and on Mondays between 2014 and the time it ended in 2017, because theaters are dark on Mondays . . .

In these various places, there was a first period—five years, from 1987 to 1992—when the seminar had a feeling of spontaneity to it as it ran through philosophy's "conditions," as they're called in my doctrine: poetry, the history of philosophy (the first seminar on Plato's *Republic* dates back to 1989–90), politics, and love. It was over the course of those years, especially during the sessions on the rue de Varenne, that the size of the audience increased dramatically.

From 1992 on, I began putting together large conceptual or historical ensembles, which I treated over several consecutive years: anti-philosophy, between 1992 and 1996; the Subject, between 1996 and 1998; the twentieth century, between 1998 and 2001; images of the present time, between 2001 and 2004; the question of subjective orientation, in thought and in life, from 2004 to 2007. I dealt with Plato, from 2007 to 2010; then with the phrase "changing the world," from 2010 to 2012. The final seminar, which was held, as I mentioned above, in a theater, was entitled "The Immanence of Truths."

I should point out that, although it was a more or less weekly seminar at the beginning, it was a monthly one for all of the final years of its existence.

II. The Seminar's Form

As I mentioned at the outset, my seminar ultimately took the form of an ex cathedra lesson, the venerable old form known as the "formal lecture" [*cours magistral*]. But this was the outcome of a long evolution. Between 1969 and, let's say, the late 1980s, there were questions from the audience. It was obviously a lot easier to entertain questions in a room with 40 people at Vincennes than in a theater with 300. But it was also a matter of the time period. Initially at Vincennes, every "class" was a sort of steeplechase in which the hedges, which had to be jumped over elegantly and efficiently, were the constant hail of questions. It was there, as well as in the tumultuous political meetings I attended, that I learned how to stay unfailingly focused on my own thinking while agreeing with perfect equanimity to answer any question calmly, even if it was clearly a side issue. Like Claudel's God, I took crooked paths to reach my goal.

I must admit that, little by little, with the "normalization," I was able to rely on the audience's increasing unwillingness to listen to overly subjective rambling, rants with no connection to the subject under discussion, biased ideological assaults, complaints about not understanding or boasts about already knowing it all. Ultimately, it was the dictatorship of the masses that silenced the frenzied dialectic of interruptions without my having to change, on my own, my relationship with the audience. In the Jules Ferry auditorium at the ENS or in the Théâtre de la Commune, nobody interrupted anymore, or even, I believe, considered doing so, not out of fear of a stern refusal on my part but because the ambient opinion was no longer in favor of it.

I never ruled out having someone else come and speak, and thus, over time, I extended invitations to a number of people: François Regnault, to speak on theater; Jean-Claude Milner, to speak on

Lacan; Monique Canto, to speak on Plato; Slavoj Žižek, to speak on orientation in life, etc. These examples give you a sense of my eclecticism.

But in the final analysis, the seminar's form, solidly in place for about twenty-five years, remained by and large that of a one-man show. Session by session, I began with careful preparation, resulting in a set of lecture notes—I never really wrote out a seminar—that provided the basic outline, a few summary sentences, and the quotations or references used. Often, I gave out a handout containing the texts that I would read and comment on. I did this because my material was nothing like philosophical references in the traditional sense of the term. In particular, I had frequent recourse to the intellectual concentration that poetry allows for. Naturally, I also engaged in logico-mathematical formalism. However, it's very difficult to make extensive use of that resource before large audiences. I usually reserved it for another seminar, one that could be called arcane, which I held for a long time on Saturday afternoons and which contributed directly to my densest—and philosophically most important—books: *Being and Event* and *Logics of Worlds*. But for the time being there are no plans to publish these "other" seminars.

III. What Purpose Did the Seminar Serve?

It's hard for me to say in what respect my seminar was useful for people other than myself. What I noticed, however, was that its transmission of sometimes very complex subjects was of a different sort from that of my writings on these same subjects. Should it be said that the seminar was easier? That's not exactly the point. Clearly, philosophy has always combined oral activity and writing and has often privileged the oral over the written, as did its legendary founder, namely, Socrates. Even those—like Derrida—who promoted the primacy of writing were very careful never to overlook physical presence and the opportunities oral presentation provides for transference love, which Plato already theorized in his *Symposium*.

But I think that the oral presentation, as far as I myself and no doubt many attendees were concerned, conveyed the movement of thought, the trajectory of the investigation, the surprise of discovery, without having to subject them to the pre-established discipline of exposition, which is largely necessary whenever you write. It had the musical power of improvisation, since my seminar was not in fact written out. I met many seminar attendees who hadn't read my books. I could hardly commend them for it, obviously. But I understood that the thinking-on-the-spot effect of the oral presentation had become the most important thing to them. Because if the seminar "worked" as it should—which was naturally not guaranteed—the audience felt almost as if they themselves had thought up what I was talking to them about. It was as though all I'd done, in Platonic parlance, was trigger a recollection in them, whereas philosophical writing per se demanded sustained and sometimes unrewarding effort. In this respect, the seminar was certainly easy, but such easiness also left traces, often unconscious ones, of which attendees who thought they'd understood everything would have been wise to be wary.

For me, there's no question that the seminar served as a laboratory. I tested out ideas in it, either already established ones or even ones that emerged during my public improvisations, by presenting them from a variety of perspectives and seeing what happened when they came in contact with texts, other ideas, or even examples from contemporary situations in politics, art and public opinion. One of the great advantages of oral presentation is to be able to repeat without really boring your audience—which would be very difficult to do in writing—because intonation, movements, gestures, slight accentuations, and changes in tone give repetition enough charm to make it not just acceptable but even retroactively necessary. So the seminar went hand in hand with the inner construction of my thought, something Deleuze would have called the moment of invention of the concept, and it was like a partly anarchic process whose energy could later be captured by prose in order to discipline it and incorporate it into the philosophical system I've created, whose final, and I daresay eternal, form, is nonetheless the written form.

Thus, some of the seminars directly became books, sometimes almost immediately, sometimes later. For example, *Saint Paul: The Foundation of Universalism* (the 1995–96 seminar, published by Presses Universitaires de France in 1997; English translation published by Stanford University Press in 2006); *Wittgenstein's Antiphilosophy* (the 1993–94 seminar, published by Nous in 2009; English translation published by Verso in 2011); *The Century* (the 1998–2001 seminar, published by Seuil in 2005; English translation published by Polity in 2007). In all three of these cases, the content of the books is too similar to that of the seminars for there to be any need for the latter to be published for the foreseeable future.

But all the seminars are in a dialectic with books, sometimes because they exploit their effects, sometimes because they anticipate their writing. I often told my seminar attendees that I was without a doubt throwing myself on the mercy of their attention span (a two-hour seminar before such an audience is truly a performance), but that their presence, their degree of concentration, the need to really address my remarks to them, their immediate reaction to my improvisations—all of that was profoundly useful to my system-building efforts.

The complete set of volumes of the seminar may, in the long term, be the true heart of my work, in a dialectical relationship between the oral and the written. Only the readers of that complete set will be able to say. It's up to you now, dear reader, to whom every philosopher addresses himself or herself, to decide and pronounce your verdict.

Introduction to the Seminar on Malebranche: Malebranche's "Political Ontology"

JASON E. SMITH

I do not enter into the detail of all this: because I take no pleasure in walking in darkness, nor in guiding others to the precipice.

—Malebranche, *Treatise on Nature and Grace*

Alain Badiou's *Le Séminaire. Malebranche: L'être 2. Figure théologique, 1986* [*The Seminar: Malebranche: Being 2. Theological figure, 1986*] represents the corrected transcript of a seminar Alain Badiou gave on the subject of Nicolas Malebranche's philosophy. As the subtitle of the seminar indicates, it was given in 1986; more precisely, the seminar consisted of seven sessions that met over the span of roughly two and a half months, from March 11 to May 27 of that year. Though the course presented a synthetic overview of the entirety of Malebranche's thought, it was primarily devoted to a reconstruction of the line of thinking presented in what is perhaps Malebranche's signature philosophical work, the *Traité de la nature et de la grâce* [*Treatise on Nature and Grace*](1680).[1]

The Seminar: Malebranche was originally published in 2013 by Librairie Arthème Fayard, as the second installment of what will eventually be a complete edition of Badiou's seminars published under the title *Le Séminaire*. Chronologically, the series opens with his 1983–84 seminar on the philosophical category of the "One" and its development in the thought of Plato, Descartes, and Kant;[2] it will continue up to 2012. The order of publication is not, however, chronological. The seminar on Malebranche is, according to the order established by Badiou, the second installment in the sequence that will constitute *The Seminar*, though it was in fact published simultaneously with the volume Badiou chose to initiate the series with: his 1994–95 seminar on Jacques Lacan (*Le Séminaire. Lacan: l'antiphilosophie 3, 1994–95*), which appeared in English with Columbia University Press in 2018.[3]

As the subtitle of this seminar on Malebranche also indicates, the trimester spent examining *Treatise on Nature and Grace* forms a part of one cycle within the seminar series, dedicated to the thought of being. This cycle examines three moments or "figures" of Being: an inaugural, "ontological" figure (Parmenides, 1985[4]), a second, "theological," figure (Malebranche), and a final variation, the modern "withdrawal" of Being (Heidegger, 1986–87[5]). This cycle can be seen, in turn, as part of a larger group of seminars, conducted between 1983 and 1987, devoted to the history of the thinking of being. This grouping includes, in addition to the cycle on Being and the seminar on the One, still another seminar dedicated to the category of the Infinite as it is articulated in the thought of Aristotle, Spinoza, and Hegel (1984–85).[6]

Readers familiar with Badiou's oeuvre will observe that the five years during which these seminars on Being, the One, and the Infinite were conducted coincide with the years, following the publication in French of *Théorie du sujet* in 1982, during which he was also composing his 1988 philosophical masterpiece, *L'Être et l'événement* (published in English as *Being and Event*).[7] These readers will also note that the transformation of the categories of the One and the Infinite are central axes structuring the radical revision of ontology undertaken in the first three parts of that same book. All of the proper names evoked in the titles of the seminars given between

1983 and 1987 will warrant considerable analyses in *Being and Event*, often entire chapters. All except one: the name *Malebranche* does not appear once in its hundreds of pages.

Indeed, in his short preface to the seminar on Malebranche, Badiou writes that this "seminar is the only one in my entire career which, from the point of view of the construction of my own system, has been of no use to me." However emphatic this claim might be, it should be underlined all the same that within the economy of Badiou's philosophical archaeology, the "theological figure of being" plays a crucial, mediating role: it sutures the power of the Infinite to the category of the One. The ontotheological synthesis of the One and the Infinite is, in this sense, the exemplary figure of what Badiou calls on several occasions in *Being and Event* "the ontology of Presence."[8] If the examination of Malebranche's particular variation on this synthesis was of no use to Badiou from the perspective of the elaboration of his own philosophical work, the *disintrication* of these two categories is nevertheless a pivotal achievement of this system. It is the foundation on which the doctrine of the event and the theory of the subject are built.

The choice of Malebranche—an author largely unknown outside of France—is indeed, at first glance, a curious one. Badiou indicates in his preface to this seminar that he initially considered Leibniz's ontotheological ambitions to have been the self-evident choice, and that the decision to devote the seminar to Malebranche was a more or less contingent one. The timing of this decision is significant. Leibniz, we should remember, was the subject of a seminar given by Gilles Deleuze just a year later, in the first half of 1987; he would publish a book on Leibniz as a "Baroque" thinker of the "fold" in 1988.[9] Badiou, in his turn, similarly characterized Malebranche throughout his seminar as a philosopher of the Baroque; in this volume, both Malebranche and Leibniz are grouped with Spinoza to form a network of paths taken in the wake of the Cartesian rupture in philosophy.

In his preface to his 1985–86 seminar on Parmenides, Badiou reminds us that this long cycle of seminars initiated in 1983–84 began at a very specific political conjuncture. This was a period marked by the victory of the Left in France, with the election of François Mitterrand: a victory that would paradoxically usher in a period of defeat and dejection for the revolutionary left and its "new forms of political emancipation." It was during this period that the Maoist political organization Badiou belonged to and had led since 1969—the Union of Communists of France, Marxist-Leninist (UCFML)—was disbanded. This was a period of "intellectual and material counter-revolution," he writes, one during which the word "communism" was not simply discredited but "criminalized," and the term "democracy" became the watchword of the so-called *pensée unique*. In the shadow of Mitterrand's triumph, much of the French Left found it opportune to renounce their own post-1968 militancy and rally to the Socialist Party and eventually to the virtues of the market and formal freedoms of parliamentarism. In this frigid climate, Badiou explains, the construction of an elaborate philosophical apparatus functioned as something of a defense, a shelter, against the chill and snap of these winter years. "Without ever giving up participating in all the localized experiments that kept the thought-practice of a transformed political life alive," he writes, "I began to build a protective philosophical shell within which it would become impossible to fall prey to giving up, let alone to be complicit with capitalo-parliamentarism . . . So, in 1983 I humbly began the journey that was to lead, five years later, to the publication of *Being and Event* by way of a fresh examination of the great history of philosophy."[10]

Though Badiou with a few of his comrades from the UCFML went on to form what they referred to elliptically as The Political Organization in 1985, this group explicitly presented itself as "post-Leninist and post-Maoist." It was founded on the premise that political parties of the type that emerged with the communist Third International were, as they put it, "saturated": finished, exhausted, through. Though this small group would produce many analyses and polemical brochures and broadsheets over the next three decades, its establishment marked the conclusion of what Badiou sometimes calls his "red years," a decade and a half during which his philosophical ambitions were largely put on hold in favor of political writing and activism. His writings between 1969 and 1982 were almost entirely publications written for and in the name of the UCFML. Many took the form of violent polemics against groups and tendencies ostensibly to the left of Badiou and his comrades—groups and tendencies he did not hesitate to tar with the brush of "fascist."[11] The publication, in 1982, of his *Theory of the Subject* marks a pivot in his work.[12] This book is thoroughly transitional in nature, more a summation and a synthesis of his thought in the late 1970s—an elaborate braiding together of late Lacan and French Maoism—than an opening onto the philosophical project that would occupy him for the next three decades.

This political and ideological setting should be kept in mind by the reader of Badiou's Malebranche seminar. Malebranche's own writing was, as Badiou underlines in the book's opening chapters, deeply marked by the "ideological and political turmoil of the age" (Session 2), with much of his published work consisting of polemics against other philosophical camps of the period, and mounted defenses against their attacks. Antoine Arnauld, for example, was one prominent and formidable adversary of Malebranche's, and appears early in Badiou's account. Arnauld, a figure even more obscure to our eyes than Malebranche, but a towering philosophical presence of the late seventeenth century—he is primarily known today through Descartes's responses to his objections to the *Meditations*—is presented in Badiou's seminar not as a singular, solitary thinker, but primarily as a polemicist and leader of the

Jansenist "party." In Session 2 of the present volume, says Badiou, "Arnauld launched scathing attacks, polemics, and questions in an absolutely nonstop intellectual activity typical of a party leader". Like Arnauld, Malebranche is himself cast in the figure of the philosophico-religious partisan. He, too, is a leader of a group or order—the Oratorians—that is not simply a school of thought but a strong institutional presence, competing with other parties for influence and leverage not only within the Church, but with State power as well. Opposed to these smaller "groupuscules" was the hegemonic "party" of the period, the Jesuit order. The great religious debates of the seventeenth century in France on grace and predestination were dominated by the radical Jansenist party and the hegemonic Jesuits, with the former condemned by the Church on multiple occasions for their positions, and pursued relentlessly by the Jesuit orthodoxy. The latter party, in its turn, had managed not only to stake out largely unassailable positions within the Church, but to position its own personnel as confessors to French kings.

The Oratorian order to which Malebranche belonged was a pronouncedly minor one by comparison. If we were to keep Badiou's own experience of the 1970s in mind here, the Jesuit order would clearly occupy the position of the French Communist Party on the Left, with both Arnauld's and Malebranche's parties situated to the latter's left. It is perhaps in this sense that the portrait of Malebranche drawn in the first sessions of this seminar has a special resonance for Badiou: it is the "committed" quality of his writing, as with that of Arnauld and others, that accounts in part for Badiou's admiration. And yet Malebranche is most clearly set off in these pages less against the Jesuits or Arnauld than that other great Jansenist of the epoch, Pascal, who plays foil to Malebranche throughout this seminar, especially in its first and second sessions, and in its very last pages.

Pascal remains a fundamental, if often overlooked, precursor in Badiou's thought: in his status as one of four French "dialectical" thinkers (alongside Rousseau, Mallarmé, and Lacan) in whose lineage Badiou situates himself, and in the place his thought assumes in the construction of Badiou's philosophical conceptuality in *Being and Event*. It is Pascal's thought that supplies the matrix for developing the two crucial subjective operators that provide the first mediations between the category of the event and the theory of the subject: intervention, and fidelity. Time and again, Pascal's name appears in this seminar on Malebranche's theory of grace. In turn, certain passages from the seminar here are closely echoed in the chapter in *Being and Event* on Pascal. The use to be made of this beautiful reconstruction of Malebranche's theory of grace is therefore the portrait it draws of a thought that shares with Pascal's the conditions of modern philosophy: the Galilean revolution in the natural sciences. Pascal and Leibniz both harbor an ambition to think what a subject, a modern Christian subject, might be in a world that is "infinite and senseless" (Session 2 in this volume).

In his response to this question, Malebranche is opposed to Pascal at every turn. It is down this path said to lead nowhere—at least for modern philosophy and contemporary thought—that Badiou wanders, and explores, on the way to building one of the most powerful philosophical apparatuses of our time.

Readers of *Being and Event* will recall not only the special place Pascal assumes in that work, but also the important epigraph from the *Pensées* heading the chapter devoted to his thought there: "The history of the Church should, properly speaking, be called the history of truth."[13] This paradoxical formulation, whose unpacking orients much of *Being and Event*'s Twenty-First Meditation, appears in the seminar on Malebranche as well, set off against an equally striking proposition in the *Treatise on Nature and Grace*. Indeed, this work's

first sentence: "God, being able to act only for his own glory, and
being able to find it only in himself, cannot have had any other plan
in the creation of the world than the establishment of his Church."[14]
As with Pascal, Badiou underlines, here "we clearly find this connection between the truth of being and the Church once again." In each
case, then, we are dealing with two variations on a single philosophical ambition: the construction of a "political ontology." In each case,
the "truth of being" (ontology) is inseparable from the existence of
the Church ("political"). In the thought of Malebranche as in that
of Pascal, being *per se* is unthinkable without the mediation of the
Church; it opens itself to thought only through the intercession of
what Badiou will refer to in this seminar in more abstracted terms
as *organization*. In the case of Malebranche, his opening proposition
means that God's glory cannot be drawn from the mere creation of
the world from "scratch." The world barely exists, argues Malebranche,
and without the presence of the Church such a world is worth next
to nothing, and exists on the "edge of the void" (Session 3 in this
volume).[15] Without the mediation of the Church, which alone attests
to God's glory, being is separated from nothing by the merest of
thresholds. For the world to exist, there must be more than the world.
There must be the Church.

But the relationship between Church and world is for Malebranche understood only *architectonically*, Badiou stresses; in Pascal's
gnomic formulation, it unfolds *historically*, "displayed or set out in
the dialectic of time" (Session 1 in this volume). "With Pascal," he
writes, "we are dealing with an historico-temporal interpretation
that validates things—relationships between the Old and the New
Testaments, retroactions and anticipations—and it is in the warp
and weave of time that this consubstantiality of the history of truth
and the history of the Church is established; whereas for Malebranche, it is not historical but structural, insofar as the Church
is a given of being itself" (Session 1). What separates these two

articulations of ontology and politics is the presence or absence of the Christian "event." Badiou reiterates throughout this seminar that Malebranche's conception of Christianity—his synthesis of the categories of Christianity and the revolution in the natural sciences, and the Cartesian geometrization of extension—avoids at all costs the specter of the crucified God, the drama of Christ's agony. It is this minimization of the event of Christ's sacrifice that cleaves apart the tragic vision of Pascal—and Badiou's subsequent reinscription of his theory of the subject—from the eventless, deductive rationalizations of Malebranche.

If Christ in Malebranche's philosophy does not play the role of the Crucified, what role does this conceptual *personnage* play instead? In this seminar's penultimate session, Badiou explores this question at length. There he notes that the *Treatise* assigns Christ two specific conceptual functions: "One can consider Jesus Christ in terms of two qualities: one, as Architect of the Eternal Temple, and the other, as Head of the Church."[16] As architect, Christ endeavors to build a magnificent monument to the glory of God; in his "zeal," as Malebranche describes it, he aspires to create a structure, a Church, with a maximal degree of beauty and splendor. This is not a physical edifice, but a spiritual one: it is built not of stones, but of souls. And yet Malebranche is eager to utilize this metaphor. The souls that are incorporated into the Church are so many "squared stones"—of which Peter was the first, after all—chosen less for their innate virtue or goodness than for their durability, size, shape, or hardness:

> For the soul of Jesus, thinking to raise a temple of vast extent and of infinite beauty, can wish that grace be given to the greatest sinners: and if at that moment Jesus Christ actually thinks of misers, for example, then misers will receive grace.... Jesus Christ having need of minds of a certain character in order to bring about certain effects in his Church, he can in general apply to them, and by that application

diffuse in them the grace that sanctifies them—just as the mind of an architect thinks in general of squared stones, for example, when those sorts of stones are presently necessary to his building.[17]

It is these considerations of structure, extent, and "infinite beauty" that, according to Malebranche, spur Christ's desire to incorporate this or that soul into the edifice of the Church; it is the aesthetic imperative he zealously pursues that determines to whom his attention turns, and therefore upon whose behalf he intercedes, so as to trigger the bestowal of grace. This process is an open-ended one, unfolding in time. Christ cannot, first of all, think of all souls at once; his thoughts are, like those of the finite creatures whom he harvests for his Church, subject to the conditions of space and time. The Church is therefore built stone by stone; it is never finished. And because many of the misers whom he elects to incorporate into his Church will be incapable of receiving his grace—their hearts are too hard, their souls too stingy—they will be rejected, cast aside. The construction of the Church entails many failures and much waste. In its margins, so much spiritual rubble.

Though Badiou would have us believe that not a trace of his seminar on Malebranche finds its way into his own systematic philosophical labors, there is nevertheless a remarkable passage from his short book on ethics (*Ethics*, 1994) that echoes this extraordinary moment in Malebranche's thought. He is considering the operative distinction in his own thought between a "subject," which for Badiou always means a subject *of truth*, and what he calls the human "some-one," any singular biological body as yet untouched by some truth. When a some-one, this or that human animal, is "convoked and seized" by a truth process, he writes, that some-one is incorporated into a—necessarily collective—subject. He or she can continue to participate in this truth only through an active "fidelity." Now, what is compelling about this passage for our purposes is that Badiou, like

Malebranche, here characterizes the hodgepodge of "human multiplicity" as so much raw material to be shaped and fitted into the "consistency" of a "subject-of-truth":

> To the consistency of the subject that he is in part become, having been convoked and seized by a truth-process, this particular "someone" will contribute his anguish and agitation, this other his tall stature and cool composure, this other his voracious taste for domination, and these others their melancholy, or timidity. All the material [*matériel*] of human multiplicity can be fashioned, linked, by a "consistency"—while at the same time, of course, it opposes to this fashioning the worst kinds of inertia, and exposes the "some-one" to the permanent temptation of giving up, of returning to the mere belonging to the "ordinary" situation . . . [18]

Where Christ as architect of the eternal Temple will unhesitatingly confer grace upon the hardest of hearts—the impenitent miser, the concupiscient, the prideful—should he judge these souls worthy of adorning the edifice he's constructing, so too the subject of truth might derive its strength, paradoxically, from the array of apparent vices that make up its raw material: the taste for domination, cowardice, neuroses, and so on. Where the soul that is incorporated into the Church is tempted by sin, the some-one who composes a part of the subject can in his or her turn be tempted: not by desire, but by giving way on his or her desire ("giving up," "returning to . . . mere belonging").

It should come as no surprise, then, that Badiou considers Malebranche's doctrine of the Church a formidable "theory of organization" (Session 6). In the passage from his *Ethics* that we've just considered, Badiou speaks not of organization but of the "consistency" of a subject of truth, a philosophical formalization constructed on the basis of a set of concrete processes: love, science,

art, and politics. However, a subject of truth in the political field is
understood by Badiou, from around the mid-1980s onward, simply
as an "organization" (as is evidenced by the name of the group he
forms after the dissolution of the UFCML). Just a few years before,
he would have spoken of "the Party," by which he meant the "party
of a new type" first conceived by Lenin at the turn of the century
(the party typical of the Third International, and embodied most
ferociously by the Communist Party of the Soviet Union in the
1930s). It is not without a touch of humor that Badiou claims that
Malebranche's conception of the Church makes him a "formidable
thinker of the Party, in the sense of communist parties at the time of
Stalin" and that his "theory [is] extremely valuable for better understanding the functioning of the parties of the Third International"
(Session 6). But in what sense?

Let me quickly sketch, in conclusion, one way to read this claim
not explicitly spelled out by Badiou. The seminar on Malebranche
not only draws a parallel—Badiou is hardly the first to establish
this connection, moreover—between the Church and the Party,
it characterizes Malebranche's ontology as a "political ontology":
being *is* truly only insofar as it is supplemented by the Church. The
world exists for the Church, just as—let us play out the analogy—
history, the truth of history, requires the mediation of the party.
The party is, in this sense, the truth of history. Now, it is precisely
this figure of the party that Badiou was taking his distance from
in the mid-1980s, indeed, at the very moment he gave this seminar. The schema of the classical Party was replaced with a subject
of truth embodied in, incorporated into a political "organization."
This theory of the subject will receive its doctrinal form with the
publication of *Being and Event*, in 1988. There, the weave of truth
and subject will assume a patently Pascalian cast. Understood in
these terms, we can say that if Pascal is the theorist of the "organized," faithful subject, Malebranche's Church is made to stand in

for the Party of the Third International. Pascal's theory of the subject proposed a dialectical composition of truth and organization, threaded together "in the warp and weave of time"; Malebranche's Church and Stalin's Party would present two figures of "political ontology," for which party and church are "a given of being itself."

Jason E. Smith
Los Angeles
August 30, 2017

About the 1986 Seminar on Malebranche

ALAIN BADIOU

As far as my own philosophical efforts are concerned, the years between 1982, when my *Theory of the Subject* was published, and 1988 were entirely dominated by the elaboration of what is often considered my most important book, *Being and Event*.

The most fundamental thesis of this book is that being qua being is pure multiplicity (the multiple without One, or, to be more literary, the multiple without qualities) and that, since the rational knowledge of the multiple is mathematics, it can be said that ontology is quite simply the science of mathematics itself.

As a result, the preliminary work on *Being and Event* took two different directions.

First, I reexamined an entire branch of contemporary mathematics that deals with sets and placed at the heart of my philosophical system Paul Cohen's remarkable conception of "generic" sets, that is, those multiplicities that have "almost" no identity of their own and are therefore particularly well-suited to supporting universal truths with their being. This work was the focus of my so-called "Saturday" seminar, which sought to develop a philosophical didactics of these difficult mathematical matters.

Next, I turned back to philosophy—ancient, classical, and modern—so as to figure out the history of the thinking of being, the history of ontology, in my own way. I took what I considered to be the principal concepts that "surround" from above and below, so to speak, the central concept of multiplicity—the One and the Infinite—and I attempted to understand the relationship that these concepts entertain with the concept of being in the different historically established approaches to ontology.

This led to a sort of rapid survey of almost the entire history of philosophy. With regard to the One, in terms of its ontological function, I studied it in the work of Plato, Descartes, and Kant.[1] The Infinite resulted in close analyses of a number of texts by Aristotle, Spinoza, and Hegel. As for being itself, I divided up its history into three parts. As far as its beginnings were concerned, I probed its properly ontological figure, grasped via Parmenides;[2] as regards its modernity, its figure of withdrawal and forgetting as Heidegger explored it;[3] and there obviously remained the theological figure of being, which was especially important since being, when conceived of as God, effects a synthesis of the One and the Infinite.

Initially, I thought that the most significant thinker on this subject was Leibniz. Then, under the influence of Martial Gueroult's enormous book devoted to Malebranche,[4] a book I'd once read with passionate interest, I went back to the *Treatise on Nature and Grace*, and I was in fact touched by something like grace. Whence the seminar you are about to read.

Malebranche is an incredible thinker, especially because, in a way, for anyone who's not a Christian, and a committed Christian at that, he seems unusable. And yet, reading him, you move from one wonder to another, as if you were visiting a beautiful church filled with little paintings, each more amazing than the next.

When it comes to the intelligibility of being, Malebranche shows unflinching courage: since God is the ultimate name of being, since the true God is that of the Christian Church, and since Cartesian rationality requires us to be able to think all of this clearly and distinctly, the fundamental categories of religion, namely, Christ and the Church, have to be categories of being itself, and we have to be able to prove that this is the case. And since the two orders of nature and grace condition men's lives in every way, in this world as in the next, their relationship has to be explained in its entirety without our ever conceding anything to the artifice of the mysterious or of the incomprehensible, which is nothing but a spiritual abdication.

Armed with a single principle, namely that God can act only in the simplest ways—otherwise he would be a capricious and frivolous creator—Malebranche sets about to deduce, yes, deduce, both Christ and the Church, as well as the action of grace, and many other things besides.

To that end, as you'll see, his method is to go straight to the heart of a problem, to resolve it, as a rule, by raising an even more difficult problem, to counterbalance this problem with an unexpectedly simple solution, which will in turn lead to consequences of a rare complexity, which will have to be dealt with by a new notion, and so on.

The result is that we've got an intellectual masterpiece of Baroque art, far more honest and pure than Leibniz's propositions. To be sure, Malebranche lacked the deep understanding of differential calculus that assured Leibniz's glory and superiority. But when it came to sincerity, to the light in which the whole enterprise was bathed, to the fluid, elegant style, to the bold conviction that was constantly engaged in his amazing proofs, Malebranche was second to none.

This seminar is without a doubt the only one in my entire career that, in terms of the construction of my own system, has been of no use to me. But it was a time of true delight, when I was able to experience, to use one of the master's terms, "the grace of feeling." I hope that you readers will be touched by it too.

Alain Badiou, February 2013

Malebranche

Session 1

March 4, 1986

Today and for the next several weeks we are going to be dealing with Nicolas Malebranche.

Father Malebranche clearly belongs to the second half of the seventeenth century. Not to the generation of Descartes, but to the second generation, the first post-Cartesian generation. He was born in 1638. He came, and this is a difference with Descartes and a number of others, from the margins of the court. His father was secretary to the King, a man of the high administration. Like many sons from this type of family, the young man was destined for a career in the Church and entered the Order of the Oratory. The Order of the Oratory was a relatively intellectual order, and rather centralized. As with the Jesuits, there was a general of the Oratory—we will see moreover that Malebranche had some problems with this general— and it was an order dominated at the time, in intellectual terms, by Saint Augustine. Malebranche was a vigorous, combative man. He died in 1715, at 77, which was pretty good for that day and age. He died the same year as Louis XIV; hence, we might say, in the century of Louis XIV.

As proof of his vitality, in late 1714, right before he died, he was still writing very significant "interventions" (this is the word he actually used), notably the *Lettres à Dortous de Mairan*. The history of these letters is instructive. Dortous de Mairan was a relatively young man at the time—he was thirty-five—and a very committed Christian. And then in 1714 he read Spinoza's *Ethics*. The reading of Spinoza's *Ethics* and the reference to Spinoza furnish an analytical framework for both the seventeenth and the eighteenth centuries. It was a breathtaking text that circulated quasi-clandestinely and that no one boasted that they'd read. Dortous de Mairan was therefore absolutely overwhelmed: the power of conviction and the argumentative power of Spinoza's *Ethics* took hold of him. He could find no objections to it, and his Christian faith was deeply shaken. He immediately wrote to Malebranche, because Malebranche had been his former mathematics tutor, to tell him about his confusion and ask him for support in this spiritual struggle. We owe to this episode a letter from Malebranche to Dortous de Mairan, in which this seventy-six-year-old man offered a well-organized and reasoned assessment of Spinoza, a judgment and arguments about the differences between his own doctrine and Spinoza's.

So you can see that, late in life, Malebranche was still fighting the good fight alongside the generation that came after him, which was already grappling with all sorts of internal problems and various forms of overt criticism of Christianity that would flourish throughout the entire eighteenth century. This incident also echoes what might be called Malebranche's own conversion. Just as Dortous de Mairan was suddenly seized and shaken up by reading the *Ethics*, so, too, it was truly through a chance encounter that Malebranche became what he became. He had been brought up in a completely traditional, essentially Thomist, philosophical framework. But in 1664, at age 26, he happened upon, truly by chance, Descartes' *Treatise on Man*. Much later on we will see that it is highly significant that Malebranche's way into Descartes was not through the front door, that is, through the *Meditations* or the great philosophical treatises, but rather through the *Treatise on Man*, that is to say, the part of

Descartes's work that deals with physiology, anatomy, and physics, too; and this is clearly, in our eyes, the weakest, least tenable part of the Cartesian discourse. Yet it was this part that completely overwhelmed Malebranche. Reading it persuaded him that his system of philosophical references and conceptions was totally archaic, insofar as a new system of reference points and figures of rationality had been developed and put into practice. It made him decide, in his own words, to "start his education anew" and to base himself on what, in his opinion, was the truth. This time around, he read for the most part Descartes—who would actually become his master, his true master—and he began to write his first work, *The Search After Truth*, the first edition of which would take him close to ten years to complete.[1]

In *The Search After Truth*, an enormous, extremely convoluted book, the first thing we find, in an as-yet not fully developed state, is Malebranche's key concept, the one from which he would never vary, and which could be called the "neophyte's declaration," i.e., his founding intuition. Then there's also a sort of incredible patchwork of reflections on a host of weird things, everything from the wings of birds to the soul of the fetus, seashells, the movements of the planets, physics, light, etc., all of it in conspicuous disorder. In Malebranche, starting with this period—that is, in the editions of 1670–1680—there was an anticipation of the eighteenth-century man, the man who is intellectually curious about everything. There was an Encyclopedist avant la lettre side to him. First of all, we are no longer dealing with Descartes's rigid and highly organized ways of doing things. Something much more freewheeling was evident, something that prepared the ground for the books that would follow in the eighteenth century. These took the form of somewhat capricious explorations of the discoveries of science, travel narratives, amusing experiences, juicy anecdotes, etc., of the "grab bag" variety that can be found in a whole slew of works, and in particular—Malebranche was clearly the precursor of this—in apologetic works. Indeed, the eighteenth century left us a large number of such apologetic works, i.e. works that defend the good cause, that of religion as such, but which do so precisely by glorifying and using the most recent discoveries and the tableau of the natural world. The classic of this kind of work is Abbé Noël-Antoine Pluche's *The Spectacle of Nature* (1732), an apologetic for the wonders of nature that sought to enlist the nascent empirical sciences (botany and so on) in the service of glorifying the Lord. A considerable tradition, and one that would continue in France all the way up to Pierre Teilhard de Chardin.

There was a bit of that in Malebranche, a side that, because it was, so to speak, ahead of its time, hurt him. It hurt him in one respect in particular, namely his inclusion in the serious and established body of seventeenth-century philosophers, such as we see them today. This hybrid side of him, at the boundary between the seventeenth and eighteenth centuries, with its blend of very great systematicity and freewheeling exploration, makes it quite difficult to assess his work in terms of the image we might have of the differences between the seventeenth and eighteenth centuries. But in what might be called Malebranche's "anecdotalism" there is something, in my opinion, more important. Unlike Spinoza, Leibniz, or Descartes, Malebranche was a priest and for that reason he was someone who brought to bear the fact that he was responsible for souls right into his conception of philosophy. In his own eyes, his responsibility wasn't exclusively the responsibility for a singular adventure of thought; it was that of someone who, being responsible for souls, had to maintain a certain connection with the masses in his philosophical message. In Malebranche there is neither Descartes's haughtiness, ultimately based on an intellectual aristocratism—which was moreover the intellectual aristocratism of the mathematician Descartes also was—nor the absolute solitude of Spinoza, a thinker who was acutely aware of not being responsible for anyone. But nor was he the exemplary man of the world that Leibniz was. Leibniz represented diplomacy, the small German courts, the comings and goings of Europeans, cosmopolitanism, plus an extraordinary art of intellectual compromise: never get too angry with anyone, especially if he or she holds an important position. And since I was talking about Spinoza, let me mention that Leibniz was someone who, first, went to see Spinoza and, second, always denied having done so.

Malebranche corresponded to none of these three figures. He was someone who was in the position of a militant and had to remain so, someone who was dealing with a mass doctrine, even if he was providing it with a new intellectuality. As a result, he was extremely attentive to what could and should be done—to how, for example, the little anecdotes of popular consciousness, broadly speaking, or those that might be going around at the court or elsewhere, should be dealt with. And so he was someone who was interested in, and discussed in his books, all the little anecdotes making the rounds. Imagine someone today who would be led, for institutional reasons, to consider it necessary for philosophy to give its view on and deal explicitly with issues like flying saucers, horoscopes, treating cancer with herbal tea, etc. Not necessarily in order to say all that stuff is true, but because he would feel responsible for dealing with the issue, since that's what some people believe—a large number of people; and number, for the militant of a large apparatus, matters. Malebranche was of course prepared to make a selection among them, but his instinctive tendency was to deal with all problems. And he usually went about it by starting from the idea that you should trust what has been said and see how it might be rationalized, rather than adopt an attitude of rationalist hostility. So *The Search After Truth* is full of things like this, such attempts at rationalization, the direct rationalization, if possible, of things that were important in his eyes, not so much because they agreed with his doctrine but because they were widespread forms of consciousness or well-known anecdotes.

So, obviously, for us today, this can sometimes seem strange. That's the second reason he was hurt by it. I'll read you a short passage of the sort that can be found right away in *The Search After Truth*, namely, at the beginning of Book 2:

> About seven or eight years ago, I saw at the *Incurables* a young man who was born mad, and whose body was broken in the same places in which those of criminals are broken. He had remained nearly twenty years in this state. Many persons saw him, and the late queen mother, upon visiting this hospital, was curious to see and even to touch the arms and legs of this young man where they were broken.

All right, the Queen Mother's visit to the broken man [*le rompu*] who was not a criminal [*un corrompu*] was an item in the newspapers of the day . . .

> According to the principles just established, the cause of this disastrous accident was that his mother, having known that a criminal was to be broken, went to see the execution. All the blows given to this miserable creature forcefully struck the imagination of this mother and, by a sort of counterblow, the tender and delicate brain of her child. The fibers of this woman's brain were extremely shaken and perhaps broken in some places by the violent flow of the spirits produced at the sight of such a terrible occurrence, but they retained sufficient consistency to prevent their complete destruction. On the other hand, the child's brain fibers, being unable to resist the torrent of these spirits, were entirely dissipated, and the destruction was great enough to make him lose his mind forever. That is the reason why he came into the world deprived of sense. Here is why he was broken at the same parts of his body as the criminal his mother seen put to death. . . . We would have many examples like the one I just reported if children could live after having received

such great wounds, but ordinarily they are aborted. For it can be said that nearly all infants who die in the womb without being ill have no other cause of their misfortune than the terror, or some ardent desire, or some other violent passion of their mothers. It has not been more than a year since a woman, having attended too carefully to the portrait of Saint Pius on the feast of his canonization, gave birth to a child who looked exactly like the representation of the saint. He had the face of an old man, as far as is possible for a beardless child; his arms were crossed upon his chest, with his eyes turned toward the heavens; and he had very little forehead, because the image of the saint being raised toward the vault of the church, gazing toward heaven, had almost no forehead. He had a kind of inverted miter on his shoulders, with many round marks in the places where miters are covered with gems. In short, this child strongly resembled the tableau after which its mother formed it by the power of her imagination. This is something that all Paris has been able to see as well as me, because the body was preserved for a considerable time in alcohol. . . . Thus, this mother looking intently and with agitation of the spirits at this tableau, it follows from the first hypothesis that the unborn child also saw it intently and with agitation of the spirits. The mother, being vividly struck by the tableau, imitated it at least in posture, according to the second hypothesis. For her body, being completely formed, and the fibers of her flash being hard enough to resist the flow of the spirits, she could not imitate it or render herself like it in all respects. But, the fibers of the child's flesh, being extremely soft, and as a result susceptible to all kinds of configurations, the rapid flow of the spirits produced in its flesh all that was necessary to make it exactly like the image it perceived. And the imitation to which children are the most disposed is nearly always as perfect as can be. But this particularly imitation, having given to the body of this infant a shape too far removed from its ordinary one, caused its death.

There are many other examples of the power of a mother's imagination in the literature, and there is nothing so bizarre that it has
not been aborted at some time. For not only do they give birth to de-
formed infants but also fruits they have wanted to eat, such as apples,
pears, grapes and other similar things. If the mother imagines and
strongly desires to eat pears, for example, the unborn, if the fetus is
alive, imagines them and desires them just as ardently; and, whether
the fetus is to be alive or not, the flow of spirits excited by the image
of the desired fruit, expanding rapidly in a tiny body, is incapable of
changing its shape because of its softness. These unfortunate infants
thus become like the things they desire too ardently. But the mother
does not suffer from it, because her body is not soft enough to take
on the figure of the things she imagines, and so she cannot imitate
them or make herself entirely like to them.[2]

There are sometimes pages and pages like that! This obviously
poses a problem. I will come back to this later, when I describe the
general scope of Malebranche's work.

What then is for Malebranche the heart of the matter? What
was the overriding motivation of his thought? His problem was
the examination of an intrinsic compatibility between the Christian religion and modern philosophy. Modern philosophy meant
Descartes, up to and including the state of the mathematical and
physical sciences at the most advanced level at the time. Malebranche took pains to show that Cartesianism, as transformed or
deployed by him, was actually the true Christian philosophy, i.e., the
philosophy that was truly compatible with Christianity. By the way,
this is a bit like the revolutionary militant Karl Marx, who proved
that the Hegelian dialectic, as transformed by Marx himself, was the
true communist philosophy. Hegel was to Marx what Descartes was
to Malebranche. As such, Malebranche occupied a very unique position in the treatment of the crisis opened up in Christian philosophy

by Cartesian and post-Cartesian, including scientific, modernity. There was a distinct awareness of this crisis, but in a certain sense Malebranche made the remarkable decision to invert its terms. The crisis was ordinarily represented as the problem of adapting Christian dogma to the constructions of the rationalism of the time. The best proof of this is that for a long time the Church itself adopted a conservative position, in the strictest sense, on these matters, that is to say, a position of suspicion and mistrust with regard to this rationalism that it could not see how to integrate into the system of ideas that it had responsibility for. In that regard, there were big problems in Descartes's work. For example, one of the more typical problems Descartes discussed at great length with Father Mesland, without making too much headway, was what a Cartesian doctrine of the Eucharist might be. Because, if matter is only extension, which is sound Cartesian doctrine, then the host is only extension. So how God could be lodged within it was an extremely thorny issue. There is no doubt that, on a wide array of dogmatic points that are crucial for Christians, modern philosophy, with its geometrization of physical space, introduced considerable problems. Malebranche, for his part, decided to invert the terms ultimately by saying that, far from being an obstacle or an antagonistic term, modern philosophy finally brought forth a philosophy worthy of Christianity, and that, conversely, Thomism and the medieval constructions were merely philosophical artifices. Thus, Malebranche came down on the side of the philosophical modernity of Christianity itself.

On this point, the most striking comparison is with Pascal. There are two key comparisons when it comes to Malebranche: the comparison with Pascal and that with Spinoza. Malebranche was torn between them. Why Pascal? Because Pascal seemingly had the same intention: what was essentially at stake in his thought was to save Christianity under the conditions of modernity. It could be said that, with regard to this problem—attempting to save Christianity

beyond the crisis, given the philosophical and scientific ideas symbolized by Descartes, Galileo, et al.—Pascal and Malebranche mapped
out two completely different paths. For Pascal, saving Christianity
required a radical change of terrain, and it was inconceivable that this
could be achieved through the mediation of a philosophical system.
There could be no modern philosophical salvation of Christianity.
The crux of the problem had to be transformed, the center of gravity had to be different: the problematic of the Christian subject
had to be fully inhabited. Pascal's question was: what is a modern
Christian subject, that is, what is a Christian subject in an infinite
world devoid of sense? That's what is radical about his question. At
a given moment in the history of philosophy, modernity revealed
quite clearly that the philosophical apparatus was not homogeneous
with Christianity, and could not be. So, as far as the phenomenol-
ogy of the Christian subject was concerned, an extreme position,
which courageously took on the world's lack of meaning, had to be
accepted. And as a consequence, analytical reason, the Cartesian
order of reasons, or even the demonstrative order of Thomism, had
to be replaced with a completely new type of dialectical reason. For
Pascal, this new reason had to take account of discontinuity, obstacles, interpretations. Discontinuity, obstacles, interpretation: these
dialectical reference points were not in the logic of the proof. We
might say that Pascal intended to save Christianity through the twin
themes of the subject and of a non-analytical reason. In this way,
he was the founder of things that modernity has not yet exhausted.
One of the consequences of this Pascalian path was anti-Cartesianism. There was no question of linking this enterprise to Descartes in
any way. Descartes, said Pascal, was "useless and uncertain."[3] He was
fundamentally useless because he did not propose an ethics. He proposed neither a doctrine of salvation nor an ethics. Since the question of salvation was the only question that mattered, Descartes, who
proposed nothing new in this regard, was of no interest. And what's

more, he seemed uncertain because his analytical rationality was really limited and was irrelevant to what mattered. Therefore, radical anti-Cartesianism and a complete change of terrain were called for, in order to preserve the chances for a Christianity on the scale of the century, i.e., on the scale of the intellectual revolutions in the century to come.

Malebranche would define a different path, a completely different one from Pascal's, even though its stakes were the same. A different wager, truly a different approach, which involved interweaving Christianity directly into the Cartesian axiomatic. It was a matter of showing not only that Christianity was compatible with Cartesianism, but that it was its truth, and that Cartesianism without Christianity was an incomplete and inessential Cartesianism. Malebranche endeavored to produce, under the conditions of modernity, a Christian philosophy that was a complete philosophy. This required—and it was to be extraordinarily difficult task—the categories of religion and theology to be changed into concepts of modern philosophy. Thus, he did away with the problem of the compatibility between philosophy and Christianity and replaced it with the thesis of a homogeneity between them. At the heart of this homogeneity was the transformation into concepts of four religious categories that in his opinion were crucial, namely: 1) God the Father, the actual Father, the God of the Bible; 2) the Creation of the world; 3) Christ the Son, Redemption; and, finally, 4) the Church, God, Creation, Christ, and the Church—all can be regarded as concepts of thought in general, not just as particular designations of a belief. We will see that this meant that Malebranche aimed, in his own way, to disrupt the Christian narrative as a story, that is to say as an effect of belief, and to change its central concepts—God, Creation, Christ, and Church—purely and simply into effects of thought. And, on that basis, as we'll see, to change many other concepts as well: Grace, and then, within Grace, sufficient grace, efficacious grace, predestination, and so on. All of the most sophisticated concepts of theology would be incorporated into the Cartesian axiomatic and, through this strange chemistry, treated from then on as concepts of thought in general. That was Malebranche's way and that was his challenge. Something very striking resulted from this, namely that the list of his works, beyond *The Search After Truth*, gives the impression of being a list of works of a theologian in the traditional sense of the term, not that of a philosopher in the modern sense. Let me just mention a few of them: *Christian Conversations, Treatise on Nature and Grace* (the one we will study), *Treatise on the Love of God, Meditations on Humility*, and the magnificent *Dialogue Between a Christian Philosopher and a Chinese Philosopher*. China, too, was a concept for Malebranche! Just by looking at these titles you get the sense of a body of Christian theology rather than of a philosophical architecture. But we shouldn't be taken in by appearances: those may be the titles of the books, but the concepts contained within them are concepts of thought, i.e., concepts of philosophy. The Church, Christ, and so on are not the concepts of a philosophy that would support religion from outside, as it were. They are concepts of thought as such. Whether you are a believer or not is irrelevant in this regard. When Malebranche speaks about Christ, he is speaking about a concept of thought, which, as we shall see, he deduces literally. Christ is deducible. Without Christ, there is no meaning, and not just for Christians: there is no meaning, period, no meaning for thought.

Obviously, this aspect of things, including the aspect reflected in the titles of Malebranche's works, led to his falling out of favor in the eighteenth century, which, truth be told, has continued to some extent up to today. Because, before long, in the atmosphere of militant anticlericalism of the eighteenth century, Father Malebranche came to be seen as a priest. And as such he was marginalized when it came to being included on the future roster of great philosophers. Even today Malebranche is very much the object of academic study.

Several important studies have been devoted to him, and he features regularly on the curriculum for the French competitive exams. But he is, as it were, not really incorporated into philosophy in terms of its attempts at innovation, that is, in terms of its creative dimension properly speaking. Malebranche exists as an object of academic study but he is very rarely a reference in the development of a work, in other philosophers' constructions. This is not at all the case with Spinoza. Spinoza, even in the most recent modernity, is a fundamental reference for people as different from each other as Althusser and Deleuze. Where and for whom is Malebranche really and centrally a reference? Little wonder that he's not, since, apparently at least, a minimal allegiance to the categories of Christianity is required to understand that this philosophy is indeed a philosophy. And it would seem that, without this minimal allegiance, his philosophy becomes a theology, or can be represented as a theology. We will deal in greater detail with this problem when the seminar really gets underway. The fall from grace was to come very quickly, beginning in the eighteenth century. But what needs to be understood is that in the seventeenth century Malebranche had a resounding success, and the path he staked out, which I summarized a moment ago, was of great interest to many people. It seemed less steep than Pascal's path in every respect. Moreover, Malebranche is a fluid writer, too much so at times, but his prose is often elegant, supple, quite charming, with metaphors, some fine turns of phrase, and some very beautiful passages. He was a public philosopher, the reason moreover being that, as the militant of a great cause under threat, he wanted to be a public philosopher. Furthermore, in the seventeenth century, the issue he was dealing with was of the utmost importance: Christianity was still both institutionally and overwhelmingly powerful enough for the question of its compatibility with the profound intellectual transformations taking place at the time to be considered a key question. Even questions like grace and predestination were questions hotly debated in the salons; they weren't reserved for a specialized elite of theologians.

Until the day he died, Malebranche was a triple success. He was a public success, a success in properly philosophical terms, and a success in high society. As regards public success, there is a barometer: the editions of his books came out at an increasingly rapid pace throughout his lifetime. What he published attracted interest and was quickly republished, so that, for a given work, there were often five, six, seven, or even ten successive editions, providing a veritable goldmine for academic specialists, since the editions were all different from one another. Because, from one edition to the next, Malebranche provided observations, clarifications, addenda, new developments, responses to objections, refutations of present and future critiques, and so on. It swelled up like a balloon, almost to the point of bursting. Whence the well-known agony, when it comes to Malebranche, of determining which edition to use. There are different schools of thought. There was one school, supported in particular by Charles-Augustin Sainte-Beuve in the nineteenth century, that regarded the first edition as the right one: afterwards, everything deteriorated dreadfully. And then of course there are those who say that, after all, the last edition is the one in which he said everything, and so on. Malebranche himself always said—as do all authors, actually—that the last edition is the right one.

Reading Malebranche is sometimes hampered by the fact that, where the final editions are concerned, the process becomes convoluted for three distinct reasons. The first is that, between one edition and another, he had to respond to the arguments and objections that came from influential people. As you'll see, the *Treatise on Nature and Grace* raised a hue and cry. There were some very powerful adversaries: Arnauld, Bossuet, Fénelon et al.—the big guns, to whom he had to respond. He couldn't bring out a new edition as if these very influential men hadn't said a thing. The second reason is that he also had to respond to the common sense objections, that is, the objections that came from ordinary people's consciousness, about which, as I said, Malebranche cared a great deal insofar as he was a man who was interested in the forms of consciousness of his readers, and of people in general. Even when it took him pretty far afield of the subject—as we saw with the bizarre passages that I read you as an introduction— he had to respond. The third and no less important reason is that he had to be very attentive to the disputes about orthodoxy. It's clear that when you are dealing with a philosophy that involves Christian categories, it can no longer be a joking matter. It is all very well to treat Christ, the Church, and so on as concepts; but these all correspond to powerful and long-established institutions, and being denounced and put on trial for heresy are very unpleasant things. They are sometimes even a matter of grave concern. Malebranche, moreover, could see quite clearly how this played out, particularly with regard to the Jansenist affair. When a combination of theological dispute and affairs of state occurred, it could lead to harsh punishment. So he also had to toe the line on questions of orthodoxy. He had to prove that he was orthodox, and do so within a philosophical apparatus that included the Christian concepts.

So a new system of justification of orthodoxy had to be found, or well-nigh invented. It was not sufficient to treat the matter schematically, since it was not classical theology. As it was a Christian philosophy, the question of orthodoxy was itself a philosophically new question. Thus, there can be found a whole new approach to the question of orthodoxy in Malebranche, practically a new concept and discourse, which is very interesting to examine closely. So responding to the disputes and exercising caution when it came to the question of orthodoxy was what most often justified the increase in arguments from one edition to the next. However, throughout all of these editions, Malebranche's great public success was confirmed, maintained, and amplified. His books were widely disseminated and discussed. Malebranche also met with a properly philosophical success, in that his great fellow philosophers were interested in his work. He was quickly acknowledged as one of the significant and influential thinkers of his time, even above and beyond his strictly public success, which, on other occasions, concerned books that weren't recognized by the philosophical elite of the time. He combined considerable public success with a well-regarded, highly esteemed, critical success among his colleagues as well. But among these colleagues, his illustrious colleagues, this esteem was usually shown by polemics, rarely by declaring that they were wholeheartedly rallying to the other person's proposition. So Malebranche encountered that mode of recognition represented by great polemics with influential people, as well as by great shows of support on one or another issue. Thus, people like Antoine Arnauld, who helped launch his career, Leibniz, Bossuet, Fénelon, and Bayle took an interest in Malebranche and studied his work with great seriousness. The debate with him was liable to deal with so many different issues that one of Malebranche's volumes is entirely devoted to his responses to Arnauld, the same for Leibniz, and these exchanges prove that he was classed among the great.

These polemics are characterized by a constant theme: Malebranche's desire to separate or distinguish himself from Spinozism, which effectively included him in the philosophical configuration. As I told you, from this perspective, the two great differences to be considered are the difference between Malebranche and Pascal on the one hand, and the Malebranche-Spinoza difference on the other. It is safe to assume that any opponent of Malebranche, and especially any Christian opponent, would at one moment or another attempt to prove that Malebranche was really a Spinozist. This is because, at the time, being a Spinozist was in and of itself quite bad. All you had to do was prove that something was Spinozist and the case was closed, because Spinoza was regarded as a latent devil of sorts in the philosophy of the seventeenth century and the first years of the eighteenth century. That is why, all throughout his career, Malebranche had to work hard to distance himself from Spinoza. This fact structured a great many of the polemics I was speaking of, in particular *Dialogue between a Christian Philosopher and a Chinese Philosopher*: beneath this Chinese philosopher the Dutch Jew could be glimpsed.

Finally, his worldly success was considerable, considerable for a priest. At the time, Malebranche was debated in the salons, and in the great correspondences. On thorny questions he was supported by significant people, such as the Prince of Condé, who was an influential supporter at the court. He also had high-society people against him, as was evidenced by the unwavering hostility of Madame de Sévigné, among others, toward him. In her correspondence, there were caustic barbs against Malebranche. This goes to show that Malebranche was much discussed in the late seventeenth century. This public, philosophical, and worldly success was for the most part bound up with the theological question of grace and predestination, that is, ultimately, with the conflict between the Jesuits and the Jansenists, an ideologico-religious conflict that was an affair of the masses in France. Take the word "masses" however you like. Let's say: the masses that can be structured by one and the same debate. But, as a matter of fact, people who were far from being specialized theologians of the court, ordinary intellectuals were all, at one moment or another, compelled to take a stand on this affair. And we will see how this sort of politico-religious conflict, of which the two organized figures were, on the one side, Port-Royal and the Jansenists, and on the other, the Jesuit order, structured some of Malebranche's positions.

Malebranche did not enter the heart of the conflict right away; he took a diagonal position, so to speak. Not a "centrist" one, properly speaking, because "centrist" would mean that he tried to avoid the blows coming from both sides, which was not exactly the case. He always faced up to the conflict when he had to, and ultimately antagonized everyone. So it wasn't an opportunist centrism, which is why I prefer to speak of a "diagonal" position. Malebranche opposed the Jansenists on the question of grace, and his merit in this regard is all the greater insofar as it was they who had given him his start. Arnauld in particular had publicized *The Search After Truth*, with the ulterior motive—as Father Yves André, Malebranche's great biographer, rightly says[4]—that it would be good to win someone as brilliant as he was over to the Jansenist party. He gave his full support to the book because he thought it was good for his own cause. Yet, even though Arnauld went out of his way for him, Malebranche opposed him on the question of grace, in circumstances that I will tell you about—they are important for understanding the work—which showed a certain courage on his part. Arnauld was an intellectually impressive figure, though constantly threatened politically on account of the monarchy's and the State's position on Jansenism. But the fact is, Malebranche ended up opposing the Jesuits as well, especially on the very important issue of the Chinese. *The Dialogue between a Christian Philosopher and a Chinese Philosopher* was very badly regarded by the Jesuits, and they devoted exceptionally hostile reviews to it in their quasi-official journal, the *Journal de Trévoux*. Indeed, it had hit a nerve. The whole affair had to do with what, exactly, evangelizing the Chinese meant. The Jesuits had a totally opportunistic conception of this. A host of traditional Chinese rituals were left intact and, save for an intermediary intellectual construction reserved for initiates, they converted the Chinese to Christianity without much trouble. It's worth recalling that the Jesuits' missionary expansion was always characterized by this tendency to respect local customs as long as formal conversions could be obtained. In the seventeenth century, the Jesuit apparatus was really the great apparatus of colonial expansion, so to speak. But this opportunism was by no means

Malebranche's position. For him it was important to know whether they were Christians, and to be a Christian a number of criteria had to be met. This idea didn't sit well with the Jesuits. That was the situation in the seventeenth century.

On the other hand, with the eighteenth century and the Enlightenment, and after these successes, this high society life, this inclusion on the roster of the greats, Malebranche disappeared from view; he fell through the trap door. This does not mean that his influence wasn't secretly maintained by a number of thinkers, such as Rousseau, for example, without a doubt. But as a publicly recognized author he disappeared, and the eighteenth-century Malebranchists were really a tiny sect, without any clout or significant influence, including in Church matters. The fate of the *Treatise on Nature and Grace* bears witness to this: after seven different editions, the last of which dates from 1712, there would be no other edition until 1837, and after 1837 none until the one we will be studying: the brave Vrin publishing house picked up a torch that had burned out a long time ago.[5]

Clearly, the main reason for Malebranche's relative disappearance from the scene was his explicit Christianity. And in addition, it is impossible to make cuts in his work. It's not like when you're dealing with what might be called theological mathemes, from which the Christian reference can be abstracted. In Malebranche, the Christian categories themselves are the operational concepts, hence impossible to cut or abstract. But I also believe there is another reason, virtually independent of the first one, and which has to do with the very form of his thought. Malebranche's thought seems torn between a core of paradoxical-seeming theses, a small core to which he is usually reduced, and whose titles are moreover extremely subversive. There's that, on the one hand, and, on the other, a host of referents, anecdotes, specific questions, citations, a sort of scattered profusion of the subject under consideration. You get the impression of an extremely fraught relationship between a small number of very strange axioms, and an excessive and overabundant, overflowing subject matter. That's the impression you get when you read him, and it is ultimately quite difficult to know where the true center of gravity is located. What is Malebranche's thought? If you take the theses—what I call the matrical core—of his philosophy, you can identify two of them above all, the ones that are in fact always mentioned whenever anyone talks about him . . . which is rarely the case. These two theses are the "vision in God" and occasionalism. It can be said that Malebranche is the vision in God plus occasionalism, in the same way you'd say, about Nietzsche's philosophy, for example, that it's the eternal return plus the will to power.

These are two extremely bizarre theses. The thesis on vision in God holds that our mind does not see, nor does it hear, real bodies. When we see a table, we do not see a table, even though it is right before our eyes; we see its idea in God, even in the act of seeing. Seeing, for a Cartesian, is an intellectual operation, an operation of thought. It is in fact only the radical consequence of one of Descartes's theses, the solution to a difficult problem that is specific to him. As you know, one of Descartes's fundamental theses is that thought and extension are radically different substances. They are two unrelated modes of being. But, if you say that seeing a real body is an actual operation, you reintroduce the relationship between them. Indeed, if thought qua thought and extension qua extension are substantially different from each other, you have to go right to the end of the argument. You shouldn't say: I can "see" or "think" a real body, because that would mean that in reality there is a relationship. So Malebranche confronted a very real problem of Cartesianism, and *he* went straight to the point by saying: thought can only be concerned with thought; it can only be related to what is homogeneous with it, and therefore when it believes it is seeing a real body, what it is seeing is the idea of this body as it is in God, for in God there are ideas of everything. Everything I'm saying here is very crude, but I'm doing so precisely in order to introduce crude Malebranchism to you. So "vision in God" is, in a way, only a radicalization of Cartesian dualism. Incidentally, this is not idealism, because for Malebranche the body is really there, it is absolutely there, since it was created by God. The problem is that if the essence of thought is different from the body, it makes no sense to say that I see it. It does make sense to say that I see its idea. Not its idea in me, for reasons peculiar to Malebranche—this is not Berkeley, it is not "there are only my ideas"—but its idea in God. The real body is simply the occasion for me to see its idea in God. Which introduces Malebranche's second great theme, occasionalism.

Occasionalism, too, is the radicalization of one of Descartes' theses, which consists in saying that God alone acts. This should be taken literally: God alone has any efficacity. For example, if you see one billiard ball hit another one, and this other ball moves, of course you'll think that it's the impact with the first ball that makes the second one move. However, this is altogether impossible, since there is nothing but geometricality in extension. The substance of bodies is extension: that is the Cartesian thesis. If all you have is extension, that is, geometry, there can be nothing efficacious. Where, indeed, can it be lodged? You'd have to introduce obscure forces, incomprehensible things. If all you have is Euclidean space, only figures and movements, how can you have energy, and therefore efficacity? There is no such thing as intranatural energy, or natural action. According to Malebranche, it can therefore only be God who makes the second billiard ball move. That's the only reasonable solution compatible with the Cartesian axiomatics. It is the only one that offers a solution to what for Descartes was an impasse, because he was in fact very much in a quandary about the problem of impact. So, when the billiard ball strikes the other billiard bill, it is an occasion for God to act. And this requires that God act, without for all that limiting his freedom. Just as, when the table enters my field of vision, it is the occasion to see its idea in God, so too, when there is a causal movement, an apparent causal relation, this seeming causal relation is the occasion for divine action. This obviously assumes that divine action in reality obeys laws. They are the laws for these occasions, and they do not shrink from the occasion. For you've got to trust; you've got to know that, when one billiard ball hits another, it will not remain in place, it will move, every time. God won't desert us when it comes to causality. He responds to occasions. Why does he do so? This is a problem Malebranche made a point of addressing, and we will see later on how he does so.

Crude Malebranchism therefore consists in these two theses: first, I see things only in God; second, God alone acts, there is no such thing as natural action, and apparent causalities are merely the occasion for divine intervention. These are two absolutely strange theses, two bizarre theses, whose mere presentation makes you and me laugh, as it did some of Malebranche's contemporaries. Madame de Sévigné, for example, doubled up laughing when she read this stuff. This laughter wasn't invented by us. Yet at the same time, the problem is that these are Malebranche's axioms, so to speak. But just because an axiom is weird doesn't invalidate it. We need to see how the system of its consequences, of its effects, gradually unfolds a coherent vision. It is nevertheless the case that, on account of their very weirdness, these axioms are already a first reason for Malebranche's being somewhat marginal.

In terms of what is, on the contrary, overabundant, the infinite number of specific cases dealt with, we clearly have what I'd call a baroque style. I think that Malebranche represents our great, baroque philosophical construction. This experimental Baroque, which is contemporary with the baroque style of some Jesuit churches, lies in the relationship—typical of his work—between, on the one hand, the ontological theses, the theses on being, which make God the sole operator of both knowledge and action and which therefore pull everything toward infinite simplicity, and, on the other hand, something that pulls everything toward the infinite, intricate and strange investigation of realities. What is properly baroque about this philosophical construction is that there's a sort of Malebranchian monumentality—quite impoverished, to be sure: vision in God and occasionalism come back over and over—that, with very simple, stark lines of force, represents the structure of the entire building; and at the same time a sort of overelaborate ornamentation represents its style. The whole formed by this very powerful, somewhat peculiar, bizarre framework, a bit lopsided perhaps but in any case amazing, and then by this profuse, extremely strange, florid ornamentation, is what produces the effect particular to Malebranche, which I call the baroque effect, and therefore a great baroque philosophy.

But once you have said as much, you are still only at the vestibule of the building. How do you go about "capturing" this philosophy? For the moment, we are only visiting it, we are only describing it. I, for one, am convinced that the ultimate meaning of Malebranche lies in the mediation of this baroque tension between impoverished monumentality and luxuriant ornamentation, and not in one or the other of these two terms. It is true that you can always say that there are details in Malebranche that are excessive and unnecessary and that the principle of the whole is quite impoverished. But his genius, the way in which his genius should be "captured," is this extraordinary sense of the relationship between the way the details are balanced out and the overall framework. His is an artistic genius, that of the conceptual artist, of the Baroque conceptual artist. To put it another way: Malebranche is one of the rare philosophers who is truly a philosopher of singular multiplicities. He is an anti-Parmenidean, someone who endeavors to think the proliferation of being under ontological laws. His thought is organized not in terms of

One and multiple, but in terms of law and proliferation, or law and dissemination, of regularity and absolute singularity. He confronts something extremely rare in classical philosophy, namely, proliferation as such—that is, the multiple as absolutely singular—and he attempts to show how it can nonetheless be subsumed under a law. We are dealing with what I would call an absolutely unprecedented ontological legalism. Malebranche thought of being in the network of its laws, being as such, i.e., as proliferation. He had the rare audacity to measure his hypothesis against any particular proposition of the world, and, as might be expected, this sometimes made him lapse into absurdity. But what we should think and honor is his audacity. Most of the time philosophers strictly limit the space of proliferation with regard to which they test their hypothesis— that is to say, they more or less set up a precoded worldly testing ground—whereas with Malebranche there is something at once naïve, baroque, and audacious, which is that every proposition of the world is an occasion for him to test his hypothesis. He shrinks before nothing, whether it be the latest publication by a Jesuit, what happens in the fetus, or the Chinese: it's all grist for his mill. But careful: it's all grist for his mill not in the sense that all he does is collect things, not even in the sense that he has to deal with everyone's form of consciousness, including superstitions, but because, in the idea he has of ontological legalism, it's necessary to establish whether any given proposition is subsumable or not. You do not have the right to cop out; anything can be a challenge by the world to the Malebranchian doctrine of being. His genius lies in treating anything and everything, and his weakness is that he does not always have the means to do so. Malebranche sometimes has his shortcomings, but his audacity is truly remarkable, and it is well-nigh unique.

We should add that what allows him this audacity, this pure audacity of confronting the chaos of the world, is the fact that he is deeply convinced that the world is organized. When I say "organized,"

I mean it in the strictest sense of the term, namely, organized by an organization. It is not mechanical clockwork: the world is organized by the Church. We will come back to this fundamental Malebranchian theme: the world is the site of the Church. This is the meaning of the first sentence of the *Treatise on Nature and Grace*: "God, being able to act only for his own glory, and being able to find it only in himself, cannot have had any other plan in the creation of the world than the establishment of his Church."[6] "Church" is a complex term signifying that "Church," as concept, should be thought as the organization of the world and that, of course, the world, the anything and everything of the world, corresponds to a hypothesis, to hypotheses. So if we can confront the anything and everything of the world, it is ultimately because the world is organized, because it is the world of an organization, even for those who are not organized. Thus, just as I was speaking about a legalistic ontology with regard to Malebranche, I think we should add that his is the sole case of a political ontology. Not an ontology of politics, but directly a political ontology, in that what sutures the law of being to the infinity of situations or to the "anything and everything" is the Church as organization. Everything obviously depends on what is meant by "organization": it has a double meaning, for everyone, and for Malebranche as well. Therefore, to think being, you have to think the Church.

In this regard, it is interesting to point out the difference with Pascal, in whose work there is seemingly something similar. Roughly speaking, Pascal claims that the history of truth is the history of the Church, and we clearly find this connection between the truth of being and the Church once again in Malebranche. With Pascal, we are dealing with an historico-temporal interpretation that validates things—relationships between the Old and the New Testaments, retroactions and anticipations—and it is in the warp and weave of time that this consubstantiality of the history of truth and the history of the Church is established; whereas for Malebranche, it is not historical but structural, insofar as the Church is a given of being itself. In particular, the big difference is that in Pascal there is a doctrine of the event, while, as we shall see, there is no doctrine of the event in Malebranche, for whom the event is even properly impossible. His conception of the role of Christ bears witness to this. Indeed, for Malebranche, the Repairer of the World, the Redeemer, Christ, was created before everyone else. His anteriority is not just a matter of his singularity, which makes him identical to God (if Christ is God he is necessarily prior to man), but also of his creaturely dimension: Christ as man, Christ in the finite becoming of God. This goes to show the extent to which it is not the evental dimension of the Fall and of redemption that is at stake in Malebranche, but an absolutely prior structural framework, of which the world is merely the effectuation. This idea that in order to think being you have to think the Church is an idea concerning the very structure of the world, which is not something displayed or set out in the dialectic of time, as it is in Pascal.

Finally, and I will conclude with this for today, I think the extreme interest that Malebranche holds for us can be boiled down to two themes that will structure our investigation.

The first is that Malebranche proposes mediations with concepts that are absolutely his alone. I call them "balancing" concepts and I will attempt to detect them, as with a seismograph. In Martial Gueroult's enormous and fundamental book devoted to Malebranche's philosophy, the metaphor that ultimately came to mind for him with regard to Malebranche's system—not to the vision he had of the world but to the system itself—is that of the clock.[7] An old-style clock, that is to say, a construction in which everything is done with weights and counterweights. Each time Malebranche introduces an additional term into his system, it throws it completely out of balance. And his way of thinking is to introduce yet another term, so as to restore the balance of the whole. These are what I call "balancing concepts." We are dealing with a mode of thought, a procedure that, in order to apprehend an increasingly proliferating multiple, does not merely subsume it brutally under the One, that does not short-circuit the multiple in a doctrine of the One or of essence, which would quickly reduce it to an essential idea. No: for Malebranche, to confront the multiple is to accept that one more term, an additional singularity, an objection, something that happens in the world, is effectively introduced, and to accept the risk that this may effectively throw the whole out of balance. Nothing can ever be integrated a priori; so he will have to carefully add a part, a weight, a comment, and something will tip over. Resolving the problem consists in finding what else should be introduced into the system, and where to introduce it, to succeed in restoring a balance. This is an absolutely remarkable schema of thought. And it is, in my opinion, the first center of interest provided by Malebranche's method and ontology. His thought process is not analytical, in the sense of Descartes's order of reasons; he does not go from one proposition to another by a strictly rational chain of thought. Nor is it dialectical in Pascal's sense. It is not a tragic thought, full of obstacles, and discontinuous; it is basically an architectonic thought, that is to say, one that integrates increasing numbers of multiplicities by restorations of balances. Incidentally, this gives it a remarkable conceptual inventiveness, despite the extreme poverty of its initial theses, because the true genius of Malebranche is revealed whenever he has to restore the balances. That is where he is truly creative, and can be captured in all his vitality.

The second theme, which I already mentioned, is that Malebranche is someone who wants to change the Christian narrative into a conceptual axiomatics. However, that's a way of disrupting the narrative. What obviously interests me is not so much that Malebranche was a Christian, hence that he was Father Malebranche, but rather the way he disrupts the Christian narrative. Nor is it what is not Christian in him that attracts my attention. On the contrary, it is the particular operations by which he disrupts Christianity as narrative, that is to say, as an effect of belief [*comme effet de croyance*]: and, consequently, the way he claims that Christianity can be exhibited as a matheme. Christianity as such, and not an abstraction of Christianity, which is too easy. You take the dialectic of the consubstantiality of the Father and the Son and you ultimately say that it's One divided into Two. In effect, when you have arrived at an abstraction of that magnitude, you can say that you have extracted something acceptable out of Christianity. But what is much more compelling and interesting in Malebranche is that he purports to change Christianity itself into a matheme, not simply the abstract or dialectical figures composed by Christianity, but Christianity in its real apparatus: Christ, the saints, the Churches, grace, and all the rest. And he tells us: it's essentially the matheme. I will therefore define his enterprise as an attempt to mathematize Christianity. Malebranche tried to do for Christianity what Galileo did for nature: that is to say, he attempted to establish the integral transmissibility of its laws. I don't claim that he was successful, but I do say that his enterprise needs to be measured against that standard. This problem is at the heart of the text of reference we'll be using, the *Treatise on Nature and Grace*, which deals explicitly with nature and grace in such a way as to show that it's not just nature that can be mathematized but the question of grace, too, hence the question of what is efficacious in terms of salvation and human action. It is ultimately the idea that Cartesian rationalism does not stop at natural effects, but can be extended to questions of action, and therefore to questions of salvation.

Next time, we will begin our investigation of Malebranche, oriented by this double series of questions. First, the balancing mediations, or what I call rationality through restoring balance, and then, second, this very interesting and important issue of the mathematization of Christianity.

Session 2

March 11, 1986

What emerged from what I said last time about Malebranche's work is that there are two somewhat contradictory sides to this philosopher, in the sense that the second is like a kind of compensation for the first. We saw that there was a sort of philosophical radicalism about Malebranche, namely, a determination to follow the consequences of a hypothesis through to the end and not let their seemingly paradoxical character stop him. The classic example is how he drew certain conclusions from Cartesianism, conclusions from which Descartes himself would have—and did in fact—recoil. I mentioned the most dramatic one: from Cartesian dualism, the absolutely heterogeneous nature of thought and extension—from the reduction of the natural universe to purely geometric extension—Malebranche drew the inexorable conclusion that there can be no relationship between our thought and sensible bodies, because to assume that there is such a relationship would be to go back on the heterogeneous nature of thought and extension. His conclusion was therefore that we have no actual communication with sensible bodies and, in particular, that when we see something, our vision is not the vision of a body, but necessarily the vision of its idea. For thought can only have a relationship with thought; what is ideal has a relationship only with the ideal, and can have no relationship with the corporeal. Whence the doctrine of the "vision in God," which is that all perception is in reality the perception of an idea in God himself, which is the idea of a body. This conclusion is obviously an absolutely dramatic one. But you can see how in a certain sense it stems solely from a spirit of rigor, a determination to follow the consequences of a distinction—be it between the body and the soul, or between thought and extension—through to the end without letting oneself be stopped by the extremely farfetched aspect of a given consequence (in this case, the fact that to see is to see in God). This is what I call Malebranche's radicalism. It is one facet of his thought.

The other side attests to a special genius. It amounts to compensating for the radicalism, compensating for the consequences, or, we might say, counterbalancing the strangeness. So in Malebranche, in a very bizarre way, there is a moderate philosopher, who is the bosom buddy of the radical philosopher. And the way he moderates his radicalism doesn't involve a dialectic but an architecture, in which compensations and counterbalancings of conceptual masses—to extend the metaphor—restore the harmony threatened by the radicalism. I spoke in this regard about an architectonic philosophy, which is built with weights and counterweights. Every time things get too farfetched, he will find a sort of opposite—or symmetrical—buttress, which restores the balance. The first great interest of this philosophy therefore lies in the study of its "counterbalancing concepts" and in the exploration of this logic of counterbalancing.

The second great interest of Malebranche's philosophy is also connected to this tension between radicalism and balance. I summarized it by saying that Malebranche was someone who endeavored to take the categories of Christianity and turn them into concepts of philosophy, to change the categories of faith into rational concepts. That was an utterly radical project, because his idea was not, as was the case with the great medieval philosophers, to buttress faith by reason. It was not a contribution of rational theology to religious faith. His project was to incorporate the Christian categories as such into philosophical rationalism, that is, to show that things like Jesus Christ, grace, the Church, divine wisdom, and the creation of the world were intrinsically conceptual operators with a universal import. And this went very far, since it went so far as to propose that these concepts could be deduced. We will see how Malebranche deduced Christ, how Christ was the issue at stake in a true deduction, in the sense that Christ was for Malebranche a necessary concept and not only, or even mainly, a revealed fact. There was, of course, a revealed fact. Malebranche was a man of the Church, an apparatchik, and so he was always careful to be in line with orthodoxy. But what he nevertheless really thought was that, more than being a historical fact, guaranteed by a Book that reveals his true nature to us, Christ was a deducible concept, a concept that could be inferred from a rational vision of being. This radicalism, which led him to change the Christian categories into concepts of philosophical radicalism— to incorporate them as such, in their religious particularity, into the edifice of reason—means that, with Malebranche, we are dealing with the truly unique case of a Christian philosophy. "Christian philosophy" must be taken as an indissoluble totality. It is not a philosophy that converges with Christianity, nor is it one that is compatible with Christianity, nor is it even a philosophy that helps the believer: it is a Christian philosophy in the strictest sense of the term.

If Malebranche is of interest to us in the logic that we are pursuing here, it is because this is one possible way of disrupting the Christian narrative, an attempt to make Christianity something other than a narrative, something other than a mere belief. Nor is it a matter of proving Christianity. It is a matter of showing that Christianity is immanent to any proof, since the categories of religion are concepts. Every philosophical proof will make use of Christian concepts. The radicalism of Malebranche's project consists not so much

in the determination to prove the truth of Christianity as in showing that the only rationality is Christian, and therefore that every
proof includes the concepts of Christianity. If the only rationality
is Christian, the essence of Christianity obviously cannot be a religious narrative or a belief; it has to be rationality itself. Christianity
stops being something that's told, in the sense of its revealed evental
dimension, and is turned into a conceptual axiomatic. It is a matter
of changing it into a matheme, that is, into something integrally
transmissible, of the order of universal rationality. This is why I proposed calling this enterprise a "mathematization of Christianity."

This extremely radical project was tempered by an utterly unique
balanced arrangement, of Christian categories changed into concepts.
The Christianity involved in Malebranche's enterprise was a Christianity already universalized in its signifying structure; it was a
mediating, tempered Christianity, in which each category corrected,
qualified, and counterbalanced each of the others. A typical example
of this would be the question of the Incarnation, the Father and the
Son, and the division of persons in the Christian doctrine. As we
will see, the division of persons was not thought as a contradiction
by Malebranche but as a distribution: it is the Son who truly counterbalances the Father. So there was no tragedy of the Incarnation in
Malebranche's work. There would be no figure doomed to the cross
in the Incarnation. The cross was of little interest to Malebranche.
His Christianity was not the Christianity of the cross, nor that of
the tortured man. On the contrary, it would be that of the balanced
distribution of functions.

If indeed we take Christ—the Christ who, may I remind you, was
a philosophical concept for Malebranche, a concept of thought—
how will he be treated? First of all, he will be the object of a deduction: his necessity will be deduced. We can already see how the
evental tragedy of the death of God—which lies at the heart of what
might be called tragic or existential Christianity—will be replaced

by a deduction, which tempers the tragedy by installing it in deducible rationality. Furthermore, and this is the second way he will be treated, Christ, as a concept, will be clearly assigned two functions or, as Malebranche, whom I'm quoting here in his beautiful language, puts it: "One can consider Jesus Christ in terms of two qualities: one, as Architect of the Eternal Temple, and the other, as Head of the Church."[1] I want to point out that all these words begin with a capital letter: Architect, Temple, Eternal, Head, and Church. Malebranche's prose makes great use of capital letters; there is clearly a link between this formal feature and the conceptualizing of the religious categories. Nevertheless, what subsists of the religious origin of the categories is the capital letter. The concept retains this sign; it is in the shadow cast by its sacred origin that it is "capitalized."

So Jesus Christ, with two capital letters of course, is the Architect of the Eternal Temple and the Head of the Church. "The Architect of the Eternal Temple" designates him as a function of the glory of God and as the ultimate cause of the creation of the world. He is, in his first function, that because of which the world functions as a Temple to the glory of God; he is the necessary mediation of divine glory. But Christ is also the Head of the Church, which designates him as the one responsible for man's salvation. This is a completely different function.

Once Christ was deduced and clearly identified in his double function, Malebranche would draw the inexorable consequences of this. And he would do so in connection with an issue that was crucial in the debate of the time: why don't some men who are "righteous," sincere believers, decent people, receive sufficient grace when they are faced with a terrible temptation? This was a question of concern to the masses in the religious crisis of the day. It amounted to asking why God dispenses his grace seemingly at random, with the result that righteous men are damned and wicked men saved. This question, which concerned the mass subjectivity of religion in the highest degree, and which therefore concerned Malebranche in the highest degree, would be treated by him in terms of Christ's double function. And it is only in terms of this functional dualism that the question of the apparent injustice of salvation would find a rational treatment.

What I wanted to make you feel in this type of debate was the very close connection between radicalism and moderation, as well as the audacious, indeed weird, nature of Malebranche's hypotheses. Yet the conclusions he drew from them ultimately resulted in a balanced treatment of the question. That's what is important to understand, namely, how, from extremely radical and farfetched axioms, he arrived at balanced solutions to issues of concern to the Christian masses of the time, solutions that would meet with widespread agreement for quite a while.

To conclude this prologue I would now like to mention Malebranche's most striking ideas, apart from the two main ideas I have just presented: in particular those that sound modern to us even through their theological garb.

The first of these is that, for Malebranche, sensible things or immediate reality must be understood not as immediate, but as a system of signs, all of which refer to a real efficacy whose name is God. Malebranche has this very profound idea that, in a way, the present world is only a figure, or even, a fiction. Reality is only a figure. This doesn't mean that it doesn't exist; for us, however, it is only a figure, and, like all figures, it must be taught; the world must be taught to us. This is quite an extraordinary idea, because the sensible world is usually the support or the immediate reference for the notion of immediacy, sensible immediacy, what is there, the "there is" of the sensible world. But with Malebranche, that's not at all the case, the sensible world is a fictitious effect of reality. The world is only a network of signs, and the meaning of these signs must be taught, as is always the case when it comes to signs. Malebranche even goes so far as to say that we wouldn't know the world existed if Scripture hadn't taught us as much. All we would know is that God exists. You can see the remarkable reversal of perspective. In traditional logic, the world exists and God is problematic. The approach to proofs of the existence of God at the time went from belief in the existence of the world to uncertainty about the existence of God, which might be changed into certainty. It was exactly the opposite for Malebranche: only God is truly certain, because he is that to which every sign points, and, being that toward which every sign points, he is truly the absolute source of every meaning effect. By contrast, the world, which appears as immediate, is in reality entirely uncertain, and God could easily have made things happen the way they happen without the world existing. For us, moreover, everything could happen exactly the way it does without the world existing. For *us*, but not for God. Whether there is a world or not makes a difference to God. Since what we see are ideas in God and not sensible things, we could, if such were his will, easily see the same ideas in God, without there being a world. But things are arranged so as to work otherwise. Why? Malebranche has his own idea about this. If we are sure that there is a world, it is because we have been taught as much. This goes to show the extent to which the world is a figure! That's the first particularly original element in Malebranche's thought.

The second idea, which is also very compelling, is dependent on the first. Malebranche will ask himself about the conditions of thought. He will wonder what it really means to think, and whether we can think being itself, being qua being, being in its originality. His thesis is that we in fact only think being itself—ontology, one might say, is innate—since we actually only think in God. Here again we see a complete reversal of perspective. We only think being, yet we always believe we are thinking something else, that is, thinking objects. For Malebranche, the constitutive process of true thought is obviously to free it from the tyranny of the object, so that it is attentive to being, so that it is oriented toward being, which is at the same time what it innately thinks. We might say that, in a way, Malebranche's ontology is subtractive. It is subtractive in the sense that we have to turn away from the object in order to think being. We have to remove the obstacle of facts since facts claim that what is actually only a figure is substance. But there are only signs. We need to call the objectivity of the object into question in order to gain access to being. It is this movement that I call a subtractive movement.

The third thing, which I already mentioned, is that organization is an intrinsic term of Malebranche's thought. It is its political side, in the broad sense of the term. There is only ecclesial thought, which means that the Church is an obligatory term of thought. In his eyes this is in no way an argument from authority. It does not mean, "You must obey the Church, think the way the Church does," for the Church—and ultimately Christ as its eternal Head—is a condition of thought itself, and nothing would be thinkable without it. The Church does not teach us true thought and false thought; it is not an operator of distinction between right and wrong, heresy and orthodoxy, etc. It is a condition of thought itself, of any sort. This will lead Malebranche to ask questions like: do the Chinese think? Ultimately, he will give a qualified yes to the question. In any case, he will rail against the Jesuits, against the Jesuit missionaries, who found it more convenient to say right from the outset that of course the Chinese think, and even to consider that the Chinese were unwitting Christians. Malebranche adopts a moderate position on this issue because, he says, "the first and the main plan of God is the establishment of his Church."[2] We shall see that without the Church we would have to think that the world was absurd. And since the world cannot be absurd, the Church is therefore necessary. I'll come back to the structure of this argument.

And finally, the last point, may I remind you, is that the religious narrative had to be mathematized. That's the framework of questions to be addressed to Malebranche, and some points on the basis of which to read him.

Malebranche would develop this thinking, organized on the basis of these fundamental intuitions and this very unique mixture of radicalism and moderation, in a certain historical context and, since he was a militant, this context cannot be ignored. It was a very strongly situated thinking, and a good deal of Malebranche's writings were in fact polemical writings, writings in the defense of his positions. It was really a politically engaged thinking, like Pascal's. Now, what were to be the obstacles raised by the historical and ideological situation in which Malebranche operated, and what particular problems or tensions would he encounter in seeking to develop this unprecedented project of a Christianity mathematized and therefore rendered universal once and for all? Malebranche was deeply aware of being the first to endow Christianity with its true universality. Naturally, he said that Christianity had always had this universality. But he claimed to be the first to truly name it. He did so, however, in a situation where there were obstacles, or even fairly big risks, to this project.

The first obstacle was that, where organization was concerned, there was a particularly significant one, namely the Jesuits. Compared with the Jesuits, the Oratorian order to which Malebranche belonged was relatively insignificant, and all the more so given that he would soon have a falling out with the hierarchy of his own order. From the organizational point of view in the strictest sense he was therefore a threatened man, because arrayed against him was the powerful organization of the Jesuit order—a planetary, missionary order that, by providing confessors for all the powerful people, secured a key position for itself. This was a result of the fact that the established tradition wanted a Jesuit to be the confessor of the Pope and thus of most of the monarchs. Through the shrewdly chosen means of the confessor the Jesuit order remained very close to the sources of power. The Jesuits constituted a powerfully structured and centralized order with an international reach, closely connected to public and religious power. Yet, on a host of issues, Malebranche was at odds with the Jesuits. He therefore exercised relative prudence and tried as best he could to avoid conflict with them. By the way, the Jesuits were the focus of great animosity across wide swaths of Christianity. We need only look at the way they began to be expelled all over the world in the following century. Their organizational totalitarianism would antagonize, and already did antagonize, many people. But they remained a formidable power, and there was no shortage of examples of people destroyed by the complicity between the Jesuit order and the authorities. Malebranche was aware of this and acted accordingly. He would only enter into open conflict with them at the very end of his life, precisely with regard to the Chinese, and would then attempt to quell the public dispute as quickly as possible. That said, had he not died, things might have turned seriously ugly.

The second problem posed by the context is that there were at the time attempts other than his own to reconcile Cartesianism and the Christian religion, attempts at once post-Cartesian and Christian. So Malebranche had rivals, colleagues, and competitors, including in the philosophical order properly speaking, who had completely different approaches from his. These included Antoine Arnauld, to whom I'll return—Arnauld, who was inextricably linked to the Jansenist party—but also, in some respects, Leibniz as well. I won't have a chance to discuss it, but you should bear in mind that the relationship between Malebranche and Leibniz was pretty funny because, for reasons of opportunism, they usually supported each other. Leibniz in particular supported Malebranche in a number of polemics. The inner nature of their systems was totally different, but they developed a very unique type of alliance. When you look at their texts closely you can see that what's involved is a sort of agreement about the words, a nominalist agreement, shall we say. Their real or intrinsic thought was very different, but they cobbled together an apparent, verbal, agreement, which each of them very skillfully maintained. It was a very different story with Arnauld, and he was to be a great opponent of Malebranche. Don't forget that Arnauld represented the Jansenist party, after all, and was also a major intellectual and religious authority, or more precisely, an authority on the intellectuality of religion. He was someone who, for quite some time, assumed a quasi-personal responsibility for elaborating a Christianity—a thinking—that was post-Cartesian and modern yet compatible with the dogma. We shall see that, in this case, too, Malebranche managed to cope with this clique of philosophico-religious opponents, powerful people who were far from wishing him well. The third problem is that a real specter, which I already mentioned, was lurking. It was not yet the specter of communism, but that of Spinoza. Spinoza represented the cursed lineage of Descartes, the Jewish and atheist philosopher who was a source of fascination and whose work was virtually destined to clandestine circulation. In the late seventeenth and early eighteenth centuries, he was an author that everyone, including the important people, read, although they were careful not to advertise the fact. Malebranche himself made sure to make the ritual declaration that he had not read Spinoza; or, rather, that he had begun to read him but had found it so impious that he gave up after the first few pages. At the time, declarations of this sort were legion because, in all truth, reading Spinoza could put you at odds with religion properly speaking. Malebranche was particularly vulnerable to this because there was a very strong tendency in his philosophy toward the idea that God alone exists. As I have said, everything is seen in God, and we will also see that God alone is cause, that is, that all causality is divine and, what is more, that the existence of the outside world cannot be clearly proven. Consequently, it was only a small step from Malebranche's philosophy to the idea that God is the sole substance, i.e., that God is the one being. So all of Malebranche's opponents would accuse him of Spinozism. As a result, he would be frowned on by the materialist, or libertine, or anti-Christian side, but at the same time he would be suspected of Spinozist, that is, atheistic tendencies by the Church hierarchy, the priests, and so on. To be regarded as a Spinozist priest was to be really an extremely dangerous, vulnerable, figure; you were at risk of being attacked from all sides. So Malebranche constantly had to clear himself of that image and prove that he wasn't a Spinozist.

That leaves the last point. For someone who endeavored to show that Christianity was rationality itself, the non-Christian peoples represented a serious challenge. This was a question that couldn't be avoided since everyone was asking themselves that question. And this last point is connected with the others since, for example, a very important aspect of the Jesuit party's activity was missionary activity in non-Christian countries. Whence the debates on China, the Chinese, and non-Christian philosophies. Clearly, someone claiming that philosophy was Christian would inevitably be confronted with the problem of what a non-Christian philosophy might be. The publication of the *Treatise on Nature and Grace*, which is our supporting text, would tie all these things together for the first time. It was the first book in which Malebranche developed balanced, original solutions to this set of questions. Prior to this—this was the status of the first editions of *The Search After Truth*—he was still primarily a Cartesian, albeit an original one, to be sure. But starting with the *Treatise on Nature and Grace*, Malebranche was truly committed to the project of Christian philosophy. The year was 1680. Malebranche would be a typical man of the end of the century of Louis XIV, and thus contemporaneous with the ideological and political turmoil of the age. The circumstances surrounding the publication of the *Treatise on Nature and Grace* were very interesting. What incited Malebranche to take such a stand, which must be seen as a dangerous one since it went to the heart of the quarrels of the age? In fact, the driving force behind it was a dispute with Arnauld. In a way, the *Treatise on Nature and Grace* could be said to be a response Malebranche addressed to him, and therefore a blow against the Jansenists.

I told you that Arnauld was the one who had launched Malebranche's career. Don't think that he did so because he thought Malebranche was someone good. No, things never happen that way with these sorts of militant, organized ventures. He did so because he saw in Malebranche a man who could be won over to the Jansenist party, which always needed recruits, defenders, and mediators, particularly among the intellectuals. What's more, Malebranche was a priest. Through him, it was hoped, an entire order, the Oratorians, might be won over to the good cause. And if Arnauld thought such a thing was possible it was because he saw that Malebranche was Cartesian, Cartesian and Christian, and he realized that what interested Malebranche in Cartesianism was the mechanical doctrine of nature. Arnauld wasn't wrong. The young Malebranche's turnabout was indeed caused by his reading of Descartes's *Treatise on Man*, by his discovery that a new rational vision of nature was dawning. The idea that nature could be represented geometrically, as it was in Cartesianism, was of tremendous interest to Arnauld and the Jansenists, because it implied that the question of man's salvation was entirely referred back to God. The questions of salvation, grace, and faith could in no way be considered on the basis of nature and the world, since the world was reducible to the geometric laws of extension. The use to which Arnauld and the Jansenists put Cartesianism was primarily the strict distinction between the orders. Nature was geometrizable, mathematizable, and so it was ultimately an intelligible and mechanical abstract concept. As a result, the question of religion and salvation was referred back to divine inscrutability. In a sense, the more you threw rational light on Nature, which is the case with Cartesian physics, the more you were referred back, in terms of man's destiny, to the unfathomable depths of God's purposes, hence to grace. The more transparent nature was, the more the question of salvation could be explained by grace. This was ideally suited to a Jansenist, who was fundamentally convinced that salvation was entirely dependent on divine grace and who railed against any compromise of faith with worldly opportunities. In other words, the mathematization of nature, of natural laws, ultimately referred the whole question of religion, salvation, and man's destiny back to the transcendence of particular actions of God. God decides on salvation, through an inscrutable transcendence that, for us, has no law, or is, in other words, incalculable. The driving force behind it all is that, at bottom, the more you think nature is calculable, the more you purify, in a way, the idea of the incalculability of divine grace. You untangle what the medieval philosophers had left in a very tangled state.

You will notice that all of this concerns ontologically, so to speak, the division between law and non-law, a question that will serve as a guiding thread for our whole investigation of Malebranche whose philosophy, I would remind you, I defined as an attempt at a legalistic ontology. It concerns it because the more the law reigns in nature—the law in the physico-mathematical sense—the more non-law reigns in the order of grace, and the more one must submit to the inscrutability of the divine plan. The matrix of this question is really the relationship between law and non-law with regard to being. The clear Cartesian distinction—the soul and the body are absolutely separate, thought and extension are heterogeneous, etc.— thus suits the Jansenist inspiration, for which law and non-law truly divide up human destiny in terms of nature and grace.

Arnauld was a man who, throughout his entire career, was aware of being a party leader and who fought on every front. His correspondence, his polemics, his writings about the philosophers of his time form one gigantic whole. Some philosophers were forced to devote half of their work to responses to Arnauld. This was the case with Leibniz and Malebranche. Indeed, Arnauld launched scathing attacks, polemics, and questions in an absolutely nonstop intellectual activity typical of a party leader, covering tremendous ground in this way. He saw the young Malebranche as a possible ally to be won over, because he sensed in him a Cartesian enthusiasm for natural, transparent, and mathematical legality, which preserved and purified the domain of divine intervention. The problem was that Malebranche would set out a completely different vision, and wouldn't pursue the path that Arnauld hoped for at all. On the contrary, he would, attempt to extend mathematization to divine action itself and would in fact approach things from the opposite direction. Instead of maintaining the divine preserve, which Descartes had prudently maintained and the Jansenists had consolidated and structured, Malebranche made natural mathematization serve as a model, as a paradigm, for understanding divine action. Instead of retaining the Jansenist split, he undertook an ontological reunification and simply proposed a mathematics of grace, that is, a balancing symmetry between the laws of nature and the laws of freedom. Arnauld was particularly annoyed since he had placed his hopes in this young man. Dashed hopes are always a bad thing, and the situation would quickly turn sour.

The feud broke out in the years 1675–1680, in the period preceding the publication of the *Treatise on Nature and Grace*, particularly since, in the period in question, Malebranche had begun to say—casually, in the salons—that what the Jansenists were saying about grace wasn't really serious. At the time, what he was claiming was still on unfounded, as yet unwritten bases. But word got around.

At first, the feud would be an organizational feud, a feud fraught with organizational significance, because Malebranche began by leading astray a promising Jansenist by the name of Michel Le Vassor, a priest, and therefore a man who was important for Arnauld and his party. The young Jansenist priest, worked over by Malebranche in a series of discussions and encounters, would be convinced and won over to the Malebranchian vision of grace to the point of renouncing his initial Jansenist orientation. In terms of organization, this was a serious matter: it was out-and-out poaching. Malebranche thus seemed like a man who had not only failed to live up to his youthful promise, but one who, in addition, tried to poach other promising youths, by winning them over to the idea that the Jansenist ideas on grace were worthless. Furthermore, Michel Le Vassor, reckless like all young people, went around saying that he had abjured Jansenism and that he owed it all to Father Malebranche, who was so eloquent about the issue, and so on and so forth. Other defectors gathered around him. Other young priests and high-society people began to think that the Jansenists' position was in fact not very tenable. Arnauld began to rant and rave about it. . . . Note that, at the time, Malebranche had not yet written anything for public consumption on the matter. Publication was still in the offing. Some mediators offered their services and organized a dinner between Malebranche and Arnauld in May 1679, at the home of some marquis or other. This marquis was eager to understand things—these questions were of great interest to people of high society, who discussed them—but he also wanted the people he got along with personally, like Arnauld and Malebranche, not to tear each other apart to the point where he would have to choose between them. So, attending this dinner of conciliation were Malebranche, Arnauld, Le Vassor, the marquis, a count, and some society people who served as guarantors, or who created, if you like, the extraterritoriality required for the negotiation. The various accounts we have of the dinner are, as you can well imagine, a bit contradictory, depending on which party they come from. The reconciliation obviously did not happen, and the dinner concluded—anyone who's ever been a militant will understand what I'm talking about—with "We need to write a text!" Malebranche would have to write a text, because, after all, there had only been rumors, gossip, up till then. There was general agreement on this as well as on a protocol (everything was completely organized): Malebranche was to write a text, the text was to be submitted to Arnauld, Arnauld would have to say, on the basis of this text, if he agreed or not and, in the latter case, he himself would have to write a counter-text. Then, it would all be put into circulation and the public, or God, would judge.

Malebranche wrote the text during the summer following the dinner at the marquis's. Unfortunately, the situation had deteriorated in the meantime. Tensions between the Jansenists and the political authorities worsened. Arnauld sensed that trouble was brewing. He had no desire to be imprisoned, and so he fled to Holland. That's where you sought refuge when the police were on your tail. As a result, the text never reached him—it would only reach him much later, in April 1680. So Malebranche found himself in the position of having submitted the text—he did what he had been asked to do—and having received no response from Arnauld. What happened? Malebranche scholars have long studied the issue conscientiously. Did one of Malebranche's followers actually arrange for the text not to reach Arnauld, with the idea that the important thing was for Malebranche to have published his text? That's one possible hypothesis. In any case, Malebranche was convinced that Arnauld had received the text (it has since been proven that such was not that case and that he had nothing to do with it). As time went by and nothing arrived, he felt slighted by Arnauld and grew impatient. In the meantime, rumors began to spread, because the affair was well known, and everyone was talking about it. It was insinuated, including within the Church, that Malebranche was defending very bizarre theses on the question of nature and grace. Malebranche wanted people to judge by the evidence, and thus for his work to come out, and this would be part of his defense. Finally, he had had enough and gave the book to an abbot, who had read it, a traveling abbot, who took it to be printed in Holland, where it would first be published anonymously. But then something absolutely extraordinary occurred, namely that Arnauld was actually just then bringing one of his countless texts to the very same printer. Arnauld, don't forget, hadn't received anything. So he arrived at the printer's only to be told that the printer didn't have the time because he had an important text by Father Malebranche that he needed to publish right away. Shocked and outraged, Arnauld demanded that the printer show him the text, and because he was someone important, the printer didn't dare disobey him. For the next forty-eight hours Arnauld immersed himself in the text of *Treatise on Nature and Grace*. Considering it a pernicious, heretical, appalling text he ordered the printer to stop printing it immediately and undertook to inform Father Malebranche that the text in its current form could not be published, that it was absolutely detrimental to the cause of the Christian religion, and so on and so forth. The printer once again complied, and a courier, a middleman, was sent to Malebranche. Most likely due in large part to the pressure his entourage exerted on him, Malebranche demanded that the printing begin again immediately. In so doing he mortally wounded Arnauld, who felt that his authority on this occasion had been openly flouted. There are texts by Arnauld in which he complains that Father Malebranche refused, with extraordinary arrogance, to defer the printing of his text. . . .

From then on, Arnauld would constantly bombard Malebranche and his work with virulent polemics. In 1683, he wrote *On True and False Ideas*. In 1685, he started in again, publishing *Philosophical and Theological Reflections on the New System of Nature and Grace*—this "new system of Nature and Grace" was obviously Father Male-branche's. This work, which was effectively intended as a refutation of Malebranche, included no fewer than three volumes, entirely devoted to demolishing his system. Malebranche would respond in turn, and his responses to Arnauld alone take up no fewer than four volumes. This goes to show how, between 1680 and 1690, there was an absolute flood of writings by Arnauld and Malebranche arguing over grace.

And Bossuet in turn entered the fray. Jacques-Bénigne Bossuet was not just anyone. He was a bishop, with links to the powerful, and it was he who was called upon to deliver the funeral orations for the highest court dignitaries. So he was a very influential person. Bossuet, too, tried to stop the publication. To no avail. The episode remains unclear. Did Malebranche expressly refuse to have it stopped? The fact remains that the powerful Bossuet was unable to stop the irresistible progress of the *Treatise on Nature and Grace*, since Malebranche was increasingly convinced of the need for it to be published. Even in his great funeral orations, Bossuet began to criticize Malebranche directly. In the funeral oration for Queen Maria Theresa, for example, a passage attacking Malebranche bears witness to the fact that any occasion was good. Bossuet declared from the pulpit, therefore, and before the whole court:

> What contempt I have for those philosophers who, measuring the counsels of God by their own thoughts, make him the author of nothing more than a certain general order, from which the rest develops as it may! As if he had, after our fashion, only general and confused views, and as if the sovereign intelligence could not include in his plans particular things, which alone truly exist.[3]

"Those" philosophers was a royal plural. It obviously meant Malebranche. Bossuet was targeting a key doctrinal issue here, to which we'll return, namely that, for Malebranche, God only acts through general will, and only makes particular decisions in exceptional cases. That said, the polemic would gradually subside, owing to the breakdown of the alliance between Bossuet and François Fénelon, in which Malebranche would be implicated.

A word needs to be said about this because it also concerns the debate. When the *Treatise on Nature and Grace* came out, Bossuet was allied with Fénelon, to such an extent that he urged Fénelon to write against Malebranche. So Fénelon wrote his *Refutation of Father Malebranche's System on Nature and Grace.* When you poke around a bit in Fénelon's *Refutation*, you can't help but be struck by his exceptional intelligence. Fénelon understood Malebranche's system extremely well, and his refutation is very closely argued and perceptive, which was not the case with Arnauld's. If this essay of Fénelon's had been published, it is the one that would have done the most damage to Malebranche. But it was not published, for very complicated reasons that have remained obscure. What we do know is that, shortly thereafter, the alliances shifted. Bossuet had a falling out with Fénelon over the question of quietism, hence over the role of mystical interiority in religion, a role that Fénelon tended to overinflate, in the opinion of Bossuet, who at that point found an ally against Fénelon in Malebranche. Fénelon's *Treatise* would only be published in 1820, at a moment in history when the quarrel had been forgotten and its protagonists long dead. This, in broad terms, was how the relationship between Malebranche and Bossuet evolved. But the publication of the *Treatise on Nature and Grace* also caused a falling out between Malebranche and his own order. The quarrel had to do with rather obscure ideas: he was apparently blamed for trying to rationalize the question of divine action. As I have already had occasion to tell you, the Oratorians' primary reference was Saint Augustine, in a mainly Platonic tradition, for which the transcendent and inscrutable ways of divine action is a crucial point. Apparently, the

Oratorian leadership criticized Malebranche for deviating from this vision of things in order to rationalize divine action. The echo of this falling out with the Augustinian current of the Oratorians can be heard in Madame de Sévigné's correspondence, several letters of which are directed against Malebranche. I cite them as testimony to the high-society debates on this question. There is, for example, a letter dated July 28, 1680 in which Madame de Sévigné writes: "It is quite clear that Malebranche does not say what he thinks and does not think what he says."[4] In saying this, she is explicitly referring to Saint Augustine, and in this sentence the most serious thing is obviously the "does not say what he thinks," because this paves the way for imputing motives of suspected heresy and Spinozism. This was indeed a denunciation, and a public one at that, because Madame de Sévigné's letters were carefully written to be circulated. When it comes to Madame de Sévigné, the notion of "private correspondence" should be taken very loosely! . . .

As one of you was quite right to point out to me, the disputes about Providence and about the ways of God ultimately have to do with History. Once the ways of God have to be rationalized, the problem of evil in general, whether it be historical evil or evil *tout court*, will become extremely acute. If God's action is thinkable rationally, this obviously raises the problem of explaining why so many appalling things happen, a question that the inscrutability of God's purposes makes it possible to paper over quickly. But if you say that divine action can be the subject of a possible calculation, even if we don't know everything, you need to be careful because it becomes a very serious politico-legal problem.

Anyway, the debate raged, and some very important people in every sphere of society—the religious orders, the court, the nobles, the intellectuals of the day—got involved in it, and it was in this context that Malebranche would have to take charge of the direction of his work. As I mentioned last time, this is what explains, in large part, why there were so many different editions. There would be four editions of the general works over the course of the first four years, and then another seven up to the end of the century. The successive editions were modified, altered, and changed, as circumstances required, which shows that these were books of activism and not just books of systematic serenity. The *Treatise on Nature and Grace* thus dealt with an ultrasensitive issue of the time, not at all with an ahistorical or side issue.

We now come to the way that Malebranche organized his discourse, the way he would frame this question. I told you that his was an architectonic thought. The *Treatise on Nature and Grace* is divided into three large parts. At the end of today's seminar I will give you the plan of the book, because I'll have to talk about method. When it comes to Malebranche, we can't work on specific texts right from the start. Because of the architectonic nature of his thought, it is impossible to avoid having a vision that is itself architectonic. We need to begin by following him as he constructs balances and counterbalances: he finds the point of interpretation in this approach itself.

So, here is the plan, the organization, of the *Treatise on Nature and Grace*, which reflects something of the way in which Malebranche dealt with the issue. The work consists of three sections, called "Discourses":

FIRST DISCOURSE

On the Necessity of General Laws of Nature and of Grace.
First Part. On the Necessity of General Laws of Nature
Second Part. On the Necessity of General Laws of Grace

Each word of the title of this first section must be weighed. You'll note, first of all, that it is an opposition between nature and grace. Then, the word "laws" indicates that the aim is a project of mathematization. It is a matter of discovering "laws" and, what's more, "general" laws. "Necessity" is opposed to the Jansenist vision, for which grace is ostensibly arbitrary and is therefore not a matter of rationality. At the base of this ontological rationality there is a doctrine of being. Indeed, he will treat the necessity of the general laws of nature and the necessity of the general laws of grace.

SECOND DISCOURSE

On the Laws of Grace in Particular, and on the Occasional Causes Which Govern Them and Which Determine Their Efficacy.
First Part. On the Grace of Jesus Christ
Second Part. On the Grace of the Creator

What is at stake in the second section is the Father/Son opposition. Malebranche will treat the laws of grace and the system of their causality. There are two kinds of grace, the grace of Christ and the grace of the Creator, which will be two organic concepts deduced by reason. Grace is no longer an exception; it can be subsumed under the general law. The occasional cause of the grace of Christ is that, as the Son, he is part of the world. The occasional cause of the grace of the Creator is Nature. So there is a symmetry between Christ, who is a part of the world, and the world. Furthermore, Malebranche gives the subjective side of the concept. For him, a concept can only be elucidated completely if we know its subjective status. Grace in Christ will therefore be called "grace of feeling," and the grace of the Creator, "grace of light."

THIRD DISCOURSE

On Grace: On the Way It Acts in Us.
First Part. On Liberty
Second Part. On Grace

The third section deals with the opposition between freedom and grace. Malebranche begins with the need for a mathematization. And the founding axiom of his entire approach is "God could only have created the world in order to establish his Church in it."[5] There is a double structure to the problem of grace. A topological structure: the question of grace has a local structure (the grace of Christ) and a global structure (the grace of the Creator). The effects of the structure are the subjective effects of the way grace acts in us.

Session 3

March 18, 1986

I ended our seminar last time by giving you the outline of the *Treatise on Nature and Grace*. I will return to this matter now in greater detail.

We have seen that Malebranche's architectonic construction involved three very clear and well-organized parts. Initially, he establishes the necessity and possibility of a mathematization of the problem, that is, a treatment of the question of grace homogeneous with the treatment of the question of nature. He will show that there are indeed two different orders—those of nature and of grace—but also that these two different orders do not derive from two different rationalities. We note here a point-by-point opposition to Pascal, for whom the difference between these orders is fundamentally a difference between the very principles of thought. We cannot think the order of charity in the same terms we think the order of reason. So for Pascal there is a break between principles of intelligibility, whereas for Malebranche there is none. The orders are distinct, but the principles that allow us to understand and articulate them are the same.

Second, Malebranche conducts a sort of study—which I called a "topological" study—of the question of grace, which leads him to distinguish between its "local" and "global" aspects. These are my own terms. Malebranche himself speaks of a "grace of feeling" and a "grace of enlightenment." The structure is double, and we must think its articulation, an articulation that must be seen as referring in the last instance to the distinction among persons in God: the grace of feeling is assignable to Christ, to the Son, and the grace of enlightenment to the Father, the Creator. The topology of grace is founded on the distinction among persons in God, and therefore on a rationalized aspect of Trinitarian theology.

Third, Malebranche deals with the subjective effect of this double structure, that is, how grace acts in us, how it operates as a factor of subjective determination. This will take the form of the problem: what is the exact interaction, in a decision, between grace and freedom?

We are dealing here with a very recognizable procedure, one we can reformulate in modern terms as follows. We are dealing with: first, the logic of the matheme, which means that grace and divine action are not exceptions to this logic; second, the examination of the particular mathemes involved in this matter, namely, the structures of grace; and third, the subjective determination. We therefore go from the symbolic to the subject, with the third movement being the real, that is, the actualization of things. Only this third movement is actually real, since it is only there that we encounter grace qua grace, grasped in its actual occurrence and not just in its principle. This general movement organizes the layout of the work. Let me remind you that the first part, the First Discourse, is "On the Necessity of the General Laws of Nature and Grace," a perfectly explicit title, and a part that is itself divided in two: "On the Necessity of the General Laws of Nature" and "On the Necessity of the General Laws of Grace."

Before entering into the heart of the matter, I would like to emphasize once more Malebranche's paradoxical radicalism. For, in the parallelism between nature and grace, between the general laws of nature and the general laws of grace, we might imagine that we will be dealing with a kind of naturalization of grace, that is, ultimately with a kind of absorption of the logic of grace into the general logic of nature. But in many respects it is the opposite. In Malebranche, the intelligibility of nature requires from the start parameters that are usually only brought into play when it is a matter of grace. But it is not a question of extending grace to the understanding of nature. It is rather that, starting with the comprehension of nature, we encounter concepts, parameters, and criteria that ordinarily come into play only when one is dealing with problems of grace, religion and salvation. In a way, the unification, the homogeneous mathematization, occurs on the basis of the Christian categories, including where nature is concerned. Rather than with a naturalization of grace, we are confronted with a Christianization of nature. The categories of Christianity have become concepts, necessary concepts, even for the intelligibility of the world. It should be understood that this thesis of homogeneity is, in comparison with our current thinking, a partly regressive movement, since it occurs not through the rational extension of the universe of nature to the universe of grace, but rather through a sort retroaction of the Christian categories on the understanding of the world itself. That's what makes for Malebranche's paradoxical singularity. But didn't a certain Marxism assert that class struggle—the domain of politics—directly affects our comprehension of nature, that there was a proletarian science? And that the categories of politics—which is revolutionary grace—retroactively clarified the intelligibility of nature? Malebranchism can be found there where you least expect it. . . .

We are now going to enter a bit into the architecture of all of this. As I have already had occasion to tell you, in a sense Malebranche's whole philosophy is derived from a single axiom, the axiom that is precisely article 1 of the *Treatise on Nature and Grace*. It is the first statement in it. Moreover, in later editions, Malebranche would write: "I have been able to begin the *Treatise on Nature and Grace* with these words . . ."[1] ("I have been able" meaning that it's after the fact.) What follows is precisely the axiom I am speaking about, that is, article 1, which I will give you again, because you should constantly bear it in mind: "God, being able to act only for his own glory, and being able to find it only in himself, cannot have had any other plan in the creation of the world than the establishment of his Church."[2] Personally, I never tire of this statement. It is truly admirable in every way. It is perfectly audacious; it is truly radical. It should be examined in detail on its own terms.

Right from the start, this axiom sets in motion the conceptual rationalization of the Christian categories. The enterprise gets underway with this statement, insofar as the necessity of Christ can immediately be deduced from it, thanks to a very simple reasoning used many times by Malebranche. The central mystery of Christianity, namely the incarnation of God on earth, and therefore the becoming finite of the infinite, is for him the first truth, the first clear principle. What is just as typical of Malebranche is that the famous mysteries of religion, run through his austere filter of conceptual rationalization, become the first principles of reason. The articles of faith that refer to an unfathomable mystery are for Malebranche the most luminous, clear, and necessary principles of reason in general.

Let's ask ourselves first of all whom this axiom is formulated against, either implicitly or explicitly. Malebranche declares that God has created the world only in view of establishing his Church. As usual, this statement is directed at once against an opportunist and an extremist thesis. In our previous sessions we traced the militant context of this whole affair enough to understand what is at issue here. The opportunist thesis is that the world as it is, that is, the world as a natural, created, finite world, the world without the Church and without Christ, would already be quite enough to glorify God. This thesis maintains that the world is, after all, not so bad, that it contains enough marvels to bear witness to the glory of God, without having to go looking for the wonder of wonders that is God himself in the person of Christ.

There's no need of that in order for the world to sing the glory of the heavens, and there is no shortage of preachers, Jesuit ones in particular, who say as much. In the eighteenth century you could hear it said that if you looked at the wing of an insect under a microscope, it was already so complicated, so subtle, so amazing, so marvelous, that it was clear that it was singing the glory of the Lord! This is what was called the apologetic of wonders, one of the great specialists of which was the Abbé Noël Antoine Pluche, who put together entire books explaining how insects' wings, fossils, and everything that could be seen through a microscope and a telescope, all of this alone proved that God was required and celebrated by this accumulation of natural wonders. This is an opportunistic thesis, to the extent that it obviously resembles the thesis that merely being a good inhabitant of this world suffices to sing the glory of God since, after all, the world already proclaims it. Therefore, if you inhabit this world properly, without committing any outrageous crimes, if you are in the natural order, if for example you are neither a deviant, nor a hardened criminal—someone who does harm to the world—in short, if you are a reasonable inhabitant of this world, you participate in the glory of the Lord. After all, if the wing of an insect sings the glory of God, I, a reasonable inhabitant of this natural universe, certainly sing it as well. This way offers many compromises, since all in all there's not much you have to do to honor God; it is enough to be of the world, to be truly and naturally of the world. Whence a whole doctrine that will consist in saying that, if you are naturally in agreement with the world, you are in good stead when it comes to salvation, and that you'd really have to commit antinatural acts, acts that violate the laws of the world, to truly offend God and be damned. You can easily recognize the thesis, the broad liberal thesis, that amounts to saying that there are certainly many elect, since that's the norm. The elect are those people who do more or less what everyone else does.

Malebranche is against this thesis. He doesn't think that the world, the world as such, sings the glory of God, and this is so for one fundamental reason: this world, however you look at it, is finite compared with God, and—this is a thinking typical of the age—to the extent that the finite and the infinite are incommensurable, the finite in no way glorifies God. That God was able to create a finite world is the least of things; it doesn't bear witness to his greatness. It is important to understand that it is this absence of relationship, this dis-relationship, that precludes any glorification. The world does not glorify God because, if it did, this would mean that there would still be a relationship between God and his creation. But since creation as such is finite, there isn't any.

This touches on a very important point, namely that the world was created ex nihilo, from nothing. This is a dogmatic point, a creationist dogma, and an argument in favor of the opportunistic thesis, which often comes down to saying that there is one thing that nevertheless attests to the glory of God, namely, the fact that he was capable of making something with nothing, which bears witness to his power. For Malebranche, this is not a convincing argument. That God can make something from nothing, that creation is ex nihilo, in no way bridges the vast gulf between the finite and the infinite. There is a very profound idea that plays an implicit but fundamental role in Malebranche's thought, namely that compared with the infinite, the nothing and the finite amount more or less to the same thing. The nothing, the *nihil* from which the world was made, from which God made the world, is not so different from the finite world itself. So there is little reason to be amazed that an infinite God created something ex nihilo, because what he brought out of nothingness, the world, is almost nothing. This shift from the nothing to the almost nothing is in no way miraculous enough to celebrate the greatness of God.

Two lessons can be learned from this. First, that Malebranche is acutely aware of the gulf between the finite and the infinite. His concept of the infinite is neither continuist, nor limited, and for that reason it is modern, meaning post-Galilean. The infinity of God is being taken in a radical sense. The second remark is that Malebranche is well aware that if you take the infinite in this radical sense, the finite is practically a category of the nothing. Consequently, creation ex nihilo is in no way a figure of invention adequate to the power of the infinite. In Malebranche's eyes, the pure creationist thesis might even mean, if you push it far enough, that God was perfectly content with creating this almost nothing that is the finite world, like a child playing at putting together simple, useless things. Far from testifying to his greatness, this thesis even undermines his glory. Indeed, to the extent that God is, as we know, self-sufficient, such game-playing is not worthy of him, and does not do justice to the being of which he is the name.

This is where Malebranche would turn against the other clique, the clique of those who, defending the extremist thesis, maintain that the creation of the world is unintelligible for man. They of course agree that the finite world does not do justice to God and does not sing his glory, but they conclude from this that the creation of the world refers to the inscrutable nature of God's plans, which is a completely different thesis. In other words, for man, the existence of the world and thus his own existence refer ultimately to the arbitrariness of the divine will, which is not an intrinsic arbitrariness, but appears as such to the eyes of men. For men, the world is contingent, and it is impossible for them to recognize within it any necessity whatsoever. This is obviously Pascal's thesis. We are abandoned and thrown into a universe deprived of sense, and so we cannot put ourselves in the place of God. We haven't the slightest idea about his calculations and we can't account for the world. There is no doubt a reason for it from the point of view of divine wisdom and will, but it is inaccessible to us. Consequently, the vision I am calling extremist here is essentially a tragic vision, whereas the other one was a relatively comic one. It is tragic because, finally, the world and our belonging to the world can only be navigated as fates, fates whose source, whose root, is uninterpretable and within which one must hope for salvation in conditions of abandonment, absurdity, and nonsense. The apologetics, to the mind of the Pascalians, the Jansenists, or the Calvinists, was no longer in any way an apologetics of wonder. On the contrary, the apologetics would begin with absolute contingency, with the fateful tragedy of our existence, in order to show that it is only by assuming an incomprehensible will, an absolute and incalculable transcendence, that effect of sense can be drawn from it. Or to show that non-sense is part of sense. But there is something irreducible about non-sense—it can be displaced, but it is always part of sense. The world has no sense; it is God who gives it one. But God himself has no sense. What I mean by this is a sense that we could master, a sense that we might exhibit or bring to light. Consequently, this type of apologetic is always dialectical, insofar as it includes non-sense in the movement of sense.

Malebranche can therefore not agree with this thesis either, an irrationalist thesis that does not satisfy the requirements of modern rationalism. We thereby see the extent to which the debate between Pascal and Malebranche became fundamental, starting in the seventeenth century. It in fact bore on the question of what was modern, that is, on the intellectual essence of the new times. It was a question that all of their contemporaries were acutely aware of. In the case of Pascal and Malebranche, the question was more precise: it was a matter of what, for Christians, was the intellectual essence of the new times. There were obviously those who would think that it consisted in getting rid of Christianity, a tendency that would be largely dominant during the eighteenth century among the intelligentsia. But, in a certain sense, this vision was a bit limited, for it would eventually be content with a combination of materialism and deism. From the point of view of the future of thought and philosophy, the more profound responses would be the ones given by those who asked what the essence of this new era was for a Christian. For, being confronted with a more radical intellectual challenge, they would have to forge and invent concepts and categories whose impact would be felt only later, even for those who would consider Christianity to be outmoded. They would invent categories of the dialectic, of tragic thought, and of subjectivity. This would entail an extremely intense conceptual and philosophical effort, because there was no short answer to the question of what it means to remain a Christian in the conditions of modern scientific rationalism.

The debate between Pascal and Malebranche dealt at bottom with just this. It is clear that Pascal's response was: modernity, for a Christian, meant tracing the limits of rationalism. It was not a matter of dragging one's feet, as the backwards Scholastics were doing, of continuing to oppose Galileo with Aristotle, and so on; it was a matter of immediately undertaking the work of limiting scientific rationalism. And that was the theory of orders. As a mathematician, as a physicist, an accomplished scholar, Pascal was nothing like a backward Scholastic and he felt justified in expressing his thoughts on the matter of the limits of rationality. He would find these limits in the concept of the subject, and he would bring to light how it was torn between different orders, the split that separated the order of reason from that of the heart. It was in the exploration of this split that he deployed the inventions of modern Christianity. Pascal and his supporters were at the root of a subjectivo-dialectical filiation, whose formal matrices went well beyond Christianity, and therefore well beyond what for them was its key issue.

Malebranche's response was diametrically opposed. It consisted in rationalizing Christianity rather than undertaking, from the perspective of Christianity, the work of drawing out the limits of modern scientific rationalism. His aim, let me repeat, was to show that modern scientific rationalism was homogeneous with Christianity. And since Christianity had anticipated this rationality—when it emerged was seen as being homogeneous with Christianity—it was possible to maintain that Christianity as such was a blind anticipation of modern rationalism. This was of course why Malebranche, ultimately, could only be hostile to the extremist solution, to the tragic solution: unbearable transcendence, nonsense as an integral part of sense. . . . In other words, he absolutely rejected the thesis of the contingency of the world. His deepest conviction was that if you do not contend that the world must have a reason, the modern rationalists will be quick to say that all of it—the miracles, the Incarnation, and so forth—are nothing but mysteries and nonsense, old wives' tales. This already anticipated Voltaire's polemic that none of it held up. So it was necessary to take the lead and show that the world, from the point of view of Christianity, had a reason, and that it was even only from the perspective of Christianity that it had a reason. This moreover allowed you to turn the question of contingency back on the atheists and libertines. Malebranche's strong position consisted in saying: I have a doctrine of the reason of the world, whereas you claim scientific rationalism. That's all very well, but do you know how to respond to the question of why the world is the way it is and not otherwise, why it exists, etc.? Absolutely not. Therefore, the one who is limiting rationality is not me, the Christian, but you. With regard to the trial of rationalism, Malebranche reversed the burden of proof. In the end, he summoned the atheist, the libertine, the nascent materialist, to sort out the questions of contingency and the absurd. Whereas he, for his part, showed that Christianity deployed a coherent doctrine of the reason of the world.

There you have in broad strokes the polemical site of Malebranche's thesis, opposed as it is both to laxist opportunism, for which the world alone suffices to celebrate the glory of God, and to the tragic extremist thesis, which maintains that there is a radical contingency. He would use all of this in arguing that the world should have a sense commensurable with God, precisely to situate himself beyond the two preceding theses. In fact, the opportunistic thesis said that there was a sense but it was not commensurable, whereas the extremist thesis said that there was no sense. The problem was that the natural and finite world did not have a sense commensurable with God, and this was so for the reason already indicated, namely, the enormous disproportion between the finite and the infinite. To arrive at a sense commensurable with God the gap between the finite and the infinite had to be bridged. Now, you can add the finite to the finite, but it will always remain the finite. The gap between the finite and the infinite can only be bridged by the infinite. Consequently, the world plus God was necessary, the world needed to be such that God was in the world, in the strict sense: not that God should remain God outside of the world, but that God should be in the world. There was a modality of the finite existence of the infinite; hence the Incarnation was necessary.

We need to look closely, beyond the apparent theology, at this ontological feature of Malebranche's thought. Indeed, there are two completely fascinating characteristics involved here. First, it is an immanentist ontology. And second, it is an ontology of the subject: in other words, being is subject.

An immanentist ontology. How should this be understood? Let's ontologize, if you will, the proposition and agree that "God" is the name of being. Malebranche's fundamental thesis is that, since being is infinite—to be understood, I repeat, not as your average theological thesis, but as a modern thesis—every effect of sense it supports, every effect of sense that might hypothetically be attributed to it, can only relate to itself. This is what I call immanentism. The radical infinity of being means that it has sense only with regard to itself. Consequently, the finite, the created, which is almost nothing—and we will see that this almost-nothing is the whole question of the other—is fundamentally a mediation of the infinite. To the extent that the finite pertains to any sense, it is as a mediation of the infinite. That is to say, in terms of its destination, through the mediation of the finite, through the mediation of the created, the infinite is directed toward itself. No effect of sense can relate the infinite to the finite as such; every effect of sense only ever relates the infinite to itself.

Now this mediation, the fact that the finite is a mediation of the infinite, is called "glory" by Malebranche. A strange name for designating the way the finite is the mediation of the infinite! And a good deal of Malebranche's explanation consists in exploring this word. It is certainly a classical word of religious adoration. But what does it mean for the mediating relation of the finite and the infinite to be called "glory"? It is as if we were dealing with the God of a Corneille tragedy, who acts for his own glory, and in particular who thus does "almost nothing" for his own glory. It is clear that, in order for this truly to be glory, God must put himself into this almost-nothing, or it won't be glorious. Consequently, the infinite creates the finite, being creates its other, but this other must include the same, because if not, the act will have no sense. If the act is not comparable to the same of being, it is deprived of sense, that is, impossible. We can therefore speak of immanentism, in the precise sense in which there is an other only insofar as the same is of this other. By the way, what we encounter here is a Hegelian theme, which is that there is no pure disjunction, and that the alterity of the world in relation to God cannot be thought of as disjunctive. The same must introject itself into the other. That is what the incarnation of God is. This immanentism is pre-Hegelian, and this is not the only time we will see affinities between Malebranche and Hegel.

Let's turn now to what I have called "subjective" ontology. The categories of decision, sense, or calculation are adequate for God. And so being qua being, subsumable under the name of God, is essentially a calculating subject. This is what Malebranche calls wisdom or order: the wisdom of God, or the submission of God to order. God is therefore a calculating subject. And since God is the name of being, we can say that, for Malebranche, being calculates. This is why he was repeatedly accused of inserting himself into God's plans, of almost taking himself for God, of constantly saying: "God calculated this, he did this, he did not do this in such and such a way, he did the best thing, etc." Malebranche was unruffled by these sorts of objections, since, for him, we actually see in God, in the strictest sense. There is therefore no mystery about how God calculates. But this nevertheless refers to something quite profound—something that would affect everything that followed—namely that his ontology was "in a subjective mode." We have to accept the principle of this. Being is subject, in this case a calculating subject, at a first level to be sure—but, as we will see, it is also subject in every sense of the term. Only, what God calculates is, in fact, himself; he calculates nothing other than himself, he is the great calculator of himself. Even when he calculates with regard to grace or the world, ultimately he reckons only with himself. Therefore, God is a subject that is, in the strongest sense, an autonomous subject. And there is implicitly in Malebranche's thought—this is obviously not how he expresses it—an extraordinary project of thinking being in this way, being as autonomous subject.

This, too, is pre-Hegelian, but perhaps in a more radical sense than in Hegel, because the word "subject" is less substantializable, less circular. And of course, as for every subject, God's desire is referable to a law. Malebranche will not hesitate to write: "Order is the inviolable law of God." You can see how far we are from the tragically capricious, incalculable, and transcendent God. We have this to reassure us: order is the inviolable law of God; God has laws. But what is profound is that he has laws because he is desire, because he is subject. And Malebranche, who is a very shrewd analyst of the subject—at the time, or a little before, they would have said a "shrewd psychologist," a shrewd psychologist of God—knows very well that to speak of desire without speaking of the law is a joke. In his own terms, there is no thought, no true comprehension, of the question of desire, even of God's desire, that does not have to refer it to a law. Lacan, for his part, says that desire is the correlate of the law. And, consequently, for Malebranche there is a deep unity between the fact that his ontology is in a subjective mode—which means he speaks of God's will, God's desires, God's calculations, etc., as if he was right there with him—and the fact that God is subject to the law of order, that order is the inviolable law of God. These are not distinct terms; on the contrary, they are woven together.

All of this will allow us to understand creative action. It becomes clear if we take up the dialectic of desire and the law from the perspective of being. Faced with God's creation, it will be necessary to consider both what is at stake in God's desire and the law that must be postulated in order to think that desire. As usual, Malebranche's analysis of this issue will be balanced and impartial. Armed with this vision of things, he will conclude that, as a divine work, the creation of the world, under the action of God who acts for his own glory, should be considered perfect. "Perfect" is another way of saying "commensurable with the infinite." Perfection is the possible commensurability with the infinite. But since all of this is "in the subjective mode," we cannot be content with considering the result, i.e., the world; we must consider the action qua action, the working action, the creative action. The subjective nature of the divine being is no doubt decipherable in terms of what it creates, but it can perhaps be even more deeply and intimately known in the creative action as such. Malebranche will therefore distinguish between two perfections with regard to the creation of the world: the perfection of the work and the perfection of making the work. Both are subject to the law, the law of order. But the second is more important than the first. The perfection of the work is subordinate to the perfection of the working action, for the work is not God himself, whereas the working action is God himself, which makes it more essential to the divine nature. Malebranche here uses—and this is significant—the metaphor of the workman, the metaphor of fabrication. Here's what he writes:

> An excellent workman should proportion his action to his work; he does not accomplish by quite complex means that which he can execute by simpler ones, he does not act without an end, and never makes useless efforts. From this one must conclude that God, discovering in the infinite treasures of his wisdom an infinity of possible worlds (as the necessary consequences of the laws of motion which he can establish), determines himself to create that world which could have been produced and preserved by the simplest laws, and which ought to be the most perfect, with respect to the simplicity of the ways necessary to its production or to its conservation.[3]

Two comments to begin with. First of all, the image of the workman is intended to establish that the excellence of being, its perfection, is ultimately decipherable in the principles of action and not in its object. After all, after fifty thousand attempts and six months, anyone can manage to build a table that stands upright, but that would not mean that he is a good workman. If someone else is capable of doing it in three hours, it's better, even if the object is ultimately identical. Therefore, in order to know in what sense God is perfect, it is not enough to consider the world; what matters is comparing

the world to the principles, rules, and ways of its creation and main-
tenance. In reality, the created world—that is to say, this material,
finite, almost-nothing—will fundamentally obey the principle of the
maximal simplicity of ways. This means that, for an overall comparable result, God will choose whatever requires the least work.
And since, roughly speaking, worlds are more or less comparable
insofar as finite worlds are all almost nothing, the principle of the
simplicity of ways necessarily prevails. The results are more or less
of the same order, that is, from God's perspective—in any case, on
the edge of the nothing. So if we compare these various products on
the edge of the nothing—what Malebranche calls the multiplicity
of possible worlds—the world God creates is the one obeying the
maximal subjective principle, the one that testifies to his abilities as
to the simplicity of ways.

This provides us with a first example of a balancing concept, one
that concerns the thorny question of evil, the eternal theological
question of evil. As usual when he tackles a problem, Malebranche
starts out by compounding it, and we have to give him credit for
that. The problem of evil is absolutely typical. What is for theologians the traditional method of dealing with this question in the
most "economical" fashion, so to speak? It is to claim that there is
nothing positive in evil and that evil is pure negation. Examined
in its being, evil is nothingness; it is disobedience, adulteration,
privation of being, etc. According to the great Platonic tradition,
it is also ignorance. No one is willingly wicked. Already for Plato,
someone who does evil does it only because he does not know the
good; if he knew the good, he would necessarily act accordingly. For
all Platonist theologies, evil is traditionally understood as a privation of being. God is therefore not responsible for it, because, being
responsible for being, he cannot be responsible for nothingness. If
evil is nothingness, it cannot be imputed to the always-affirmative

movement of God, since God is the plenitude of being, including in his creation. In the old debate concerning the question of how to clear God of all responsibility for evil, this is the economical way of treating it. Starting from the intrinsic analysis of the essence of evil, you show that it is non-being, and for this very reason, God is absolved of all responsibility for it. What I am calling Malebranche's exacerbation of a problem stems from the fact that he is never satisfied with this type of reduction. For him, evil is positive, and an evil action is an action that exists just as much as a good one. He refuses the convenience of the detour via non-being. There really are, in actual fact, things that are bad for man. There is evil, and this "there is" is a real "there is"—it is not a privation, a negation, a partial nothingness. As a result, he has to find what I have been calling "balancing" mediations on this issue. For we are on the verge of a total breakdown here. If evil is real, God is necessarily responsible for it; but how can he be responsible for evil without forfeiting his perfection? Malebranche's answer is that the creation of the world has its founding perfection in the creative gesture, and not in its result. He recognizes very well that there is evil and that nothing is easier than identifying an objective imperfection in the world, but what must be understood is that the world contains only the evil made necessary by the perfection of creation. The creative gesture, which must obey the simplest possible laws, entails imperfections in the result—imperfections that God could of course make up for, but it would be at the price of an imperfection in his action.

Note that what underlies this, broadly speaking, is an aesthetic metaphor. Malebranche's ontology is an aesthetics of being. Let's read what he writes in one of the innumerable texts he devotes to the question: "God could, no doubt, make a world more perfect than the one in which we live."[4] That's the exacerbation of the problem: God could have made a more perfect world. He does not say: God made a perfect world, and all the evil in that world is a form of non-being. Let me continue:

> God could, no doubt, make a world more perfect than the one in which we live. He could, for example, make it such that rain, which serves to make the earth fruitful, fall more regularly on cultivated ground than in the sea, where it is unnecessary. But in order to make this more perfect world, it would have been necessary that he have changed the simplicity of his ways, and that he have multiplied the laws of the communication of motion, through which our world exists: and then there would no longer be that proportion between the action of God and his work, which is necessary in order to determine an infinitely wise being to act; or at least there would not have been the same proportion between the activity of God and this so-perfect world, as between the laws of nature and the world in which we live; for our world, however imperfect one wishes to imagine it, is based on laws of motion which are so simple and so natural that it is perfectly worthy of the infinite wisdom of its author.[5]

In this aesthetic ontology, the balancing mediation consists in compensating for the particular objectivity of evil with the general value of the act. Subjective and practical perfection prevails over the particularities of the result. I'd like to point out in passing that the image of rain is absolutely essential and recurs constantly in Malebranche, especially in the *Treatise on Nature and Grace*, where we find two great images, that of rain and that of the temple. The rain will represent everything that can be characterized as particular phenomena in the world. It is the image, the metaphor of the distribution of things in the world, and it will also be the metaphor of the distribution of grace. And there we have a strict parallelism, for the natural problem of "Where does the rain fall?" there will be the supernatural problem of "Where does grace fall?" And just as rain falls on the sea and not only over cultivated ground, so too a vile person might receive sufficient grace while a good man might receive nothing at all. The metaphor of rain is generally the metaphor of apparent disorder, that is, in reality, of the appearance of contingency in this world that is, itself, not contingent. Malebranche's adherence to the mass line can be recognized here. That the weather, meteorology, is the figure of contingency is something any ordinary conversation teaches us, and choosing this metaphor in an overwhelmingly peasant culture, as France was at the time, is an undeniable element of communication with popular consciousness. It is completely in keeping with Malebranche's particular genius.

The other metaphor is the temple, and it's the opposite of the rain metaphor. The temple, with its ornaments, is architectonic perfection. It is the baroque church, the church in the sense of a religious building. It represents the other aspect of things, the ecclesial aspect, the necessary and glorious aspect. Just as there is a dialectic of the rain, the dialectic of the place where it falls, so too there is a dialectic of the temple, of the simplicity of its architecture and its ornamental profusion. The apparent disorder is an effect of the law of order to which the creative gesture is subject. It is a particular disorder, not an intrinsic one, and it cannot be attributed to divine wisdom. As wisdom, divine wisdom has to accept the predominance of the gesture over the work, for the gesture is this wisdom itself. Here, too, we have an application of the maxim to the effect that God acts only with regard to himself: his creative gesture is predominant over the work. Therefore, order properly speaking, i.e., the infinite order, is inherent in the creative gesture. The particular disorder in the work, as a result of the order of the gesture, is only a disorder for us. We encounter once again the aesthetic metaphor. At bottom, what Malebranche says is this: when we look at the world, we are ignorant spectators. And if we are led to say: there's something off there, there's something ugly there, there's something sullied there, it is only because we do not understand the ultimate unifying principle of it all. If we understood that this fault is only the particular result of a general equilibrium, which is related to the essence of the gesture, then we could only admire it, including the evil. We would then become cultured people who are no longer taken aback by dissonance. We would know that this dissonance is merely the particular price to be paid for general perfection, not the perfection of the finished product, but of the principles that give rise to it—that is, by which it is and subsists.

So, there is ultimately only one unconditioned principle, one inviolable law of God. This unconditioned principle is the simplicity of ways. Anyone who produces effects by ways that are too complicated, that is, without thinkable proportions between the effect and these laws, is imperfect in his own order. In the case of God, his own order is the creation of the world. There are not many competitors, there is only one who, in Malebranche's eyes, is a very harsh judge of himself and constantly judges the aesthetic perfection of the gesture by the criterion of the simplicity of ways. We could also express this in the following way: the being-subject acts in accordance with general wills, that is, in accordance with a practical universalism. It limits as much as possible particular wills, because they are only adjustments, imperfect and irrational things. As a result, even the apparent particular imperfections lend support to this practical universalism. It could be said about creation what Mao said about the revolution: "The creation of the world is not a dinner party." The most important thing is that the creation of the world be commensurable with divine infinity. So we won't object to this that there are some unfortunate people who do not receive their salvation or that the rain falls on the sea. If the general principle of the simplicity of ways—that is, of the perfection of the gesture— is predominant, and if the realization of this principle necessarily entails negative particularities, these negative particularities will pose no objection to practical universalism. They are its actualization and, as even Malebranche says, they contribute to its beauty. Here is the passage:

> If then it is true that the general cause ought not to produce his work by particular wills, and that God had to establish certain laws of the communication of motion which are constant and invariable, through whose efficacy he foresaw that the world could subsist such as we see it, one can say in a very true sense that God wishes that all his creatures be perfect; that he wills not at all that children perish in the womb of their mothers; that he does not love monsters; that he did not make the laws of nature to engender them; and that if he had been able (by equally simple ways) to make and to preserve a more perfect world, he would never have established any laws, of which so great a number of monsters are necessary consequences; but that it would have been unworthy of his wisdom to multiply his wills in order to stop certain particular disorders, which even constitute a kind of beauty in the universe.[6]

The root of all of this is that, if the infinite is a subject, in this case a creative subject, it is not possible for its maxim to be a particular will, because a particular will would mean constantly correcting the bad particularities of the world, and that would tie the infinite once again to the finite. That's an argument directed against the extremist theses, the theses on contingency and the irrational and constant intervention of God. Therefore, for an autonomous subject—and an infinite subject can only be thought by Malebranche as an autonomous subject—the maxim is to act in accordance with universal wills. Incidentally, note the proximity to the Kantian categorical imperative here. The Kantian categorical imperative orders us always to act as if the maxims of action were universal laws of nature. The principle of practical universalism is a crucial principle of Kantian ethics.

We could therefore say that Malebranche's God is also a moral God in Kant's terms, namely, a God who acts in accordance with universal maxims. And this practical universalism is compossible with particular disorders.

We can therefore know that the world is as perfect as it can be, given that God acts in accordance with laws—that is, given that God desires the world. Don't think the world is imperfect because God doesn't care about it. We might be tempted to say: God is indifferent: he acts in accordance with general wills, and he could not care less what happens afterward. That would be the commonsense objection. But, as usual, this objection is inverted by Malebranche, who says that the exact opposite is true. What's needed is to take seriously the fact that the world has no sense unless such is God's desire, and also that to the extent that creation is not a whim, inexplicable contingency, sheer nonsense, it is because it can be linked to God as subject. Now if God desires the world, we can make sense of this only if there are laws, and since these are laws for the infinite, they are general laws, universal laws. Malebranche understood perfectly well this strange but true point: to think that God acts by particular will, and therefore that he constantly meddles in everything, is actually to suppress him as a subject, whereas to think him profoundly as a subject is necessarily to think him in relation to a law. Not the law that he promulgates, but the law that he, in a certain sense, obeys: the law of his desire.

What Malebranche will undertake, now that the general framework has been constructed, is to show that these principles can be extended to the questions of salvation and grace. Before we get to that, I would like to give you two additional examples of what I call the balancing resolution of problems. We will begin today with his methodology that is characterized by exacerbation, followed by a balancing out.

The first important problem, which follows from what I just said, can be formulated like this: let's assume that the Incarnation, Christ, is the sense of the world, which amounts to changing Christ into a concept and Christianity into philosophy. If Christ embodies God's plan in creating the world, God therefore created the world solely so that Christ could be incarnated in it, for that alone was commensurate with his glory. How can we understand, then, that Christ as Redeemer, as the one who saves mankind from original sin, is abandoned to the Fall, that is, to human sinfulness, to Adam's sin? How can we do so without thinking that God wanted or willed the Fall, that he willed original sin? Remember that in Christian theology the Redeemer comes in order to raise mankind from its original lapse. Therefore, if God's plan is redemption, hence Christ, then God's plan is also the Fall. The problem has to do with God's plans, for the crime is humanity's as a whole, and original sin, permanently transmissible, represents the corruption of the world whose heart is man. Could God have willed the world to be corrupt, in order to then redeem it from this corruption? This would be, at the very least, a cynical calculation, making humanity in a certain sense a victim in the service of God's glory. Malebranche does not completely shrink from this vision of things. That is the first problem.

But there is another problem, one that concerns the question of being and the event. There is eventness in Christianity, for if redemption, i.e., Christ's incarnation, stems from mankind's fall and Adam's sin, and if Adam freely sinned—we relieve God of responsibility by saying: Adam sinned, but he could have not sinned—the result is that the Redemption was not calculable. It depends on the Fall's singular uniqueness. The strict orthodox doctrine says that God's benevolence consisted in sending a Messiah, a Redeemer, to relieve and raise up mankind from its fall—a fall that mankind went through by turning away from God, hence freely. In a way, an intervening event, a temporal inscription, then took place in the heart of Christianity: the Redemption, the coming of Christ, was the evental sense given by God to another event, mankind's fall. As a result, one has the impression that Christianity is also a historicity, a divine intervention, a will to save man at the point of his fall and his abandonment. But if Christ is the ultimate sense of the world, this eventness is dissolved; there is no longer that act by which God relieves and lifts up mankind by sacrificing himself. There is instead a general calculation, in which the Fall is only one element, one moment, itself calculable. In summary, there are two problems. 1) Is God responsible for the Fall? Did he will original sin and mankind's corruption? And: 2) Should Christianity be totally de-eventalized, dehistoricized?

With regard to these problems, Malebranche proceeds as he always does. Rejecting every mediating or intermediary solution, he begins by exacerbating the problem, and does so in two ways. First, he expressly posits that Jesus Christ is the first-born of creatures, and therefore that he precedes humanity. In the process, he clearly materializes the strategic function of Christ. For example, he writes: "Jesus Christ . . . is the first-born of created beings, it is he who is their exemplar in the eternal plan of his Father,"[7] or, elsewhere and more radically: "Jesus Christ . . . is the beginning of the ways of the Lord."[8] He therefore totally assumes that Christ is the inaugural term. The de-eventalization and the anticipatory character of Christ, including of Christ as a creature, are affirmed. Indeed, it is not a matter of Christ as a project or a concept, but of Christ insofar as he was created before mankind. This goes to show the extent to which he is not dependent on the eventness of the Fall.

And then Malebranche exacerbates the problem even more by emphasizing that Christ derives from a different type of causality than the world vis-à-vis God. This point is related to the distinction between external and internal cause. He thus writes: "God, by the creation of the world, takes leave of himself so to speak."[9] Therefore, even if it is ultimately a mediation, the world is in a position of external creation, whereas, concerning Christ, Malebranche speaks of the "immanent operations by which the Son is constantly engendered."[10] Christ not only anticipates the world but, in addition, the causality that engenders him is heterogeneous to the world's causality, insofar as, for God, the world involves a taking leave of self, whereas Christ involves an immanent operation. And yet Christ is also God incarnate, therefore Christ is of the world. Here, we are caught up in an utterly extraordinary tension.

How does Malebranche balance all of this out, after having stretched the problem to its limit? Here again, in two different ways. We know that, in creating the world, being takes leave of itself in the finite—to borrow Malebranche's formulation—exclusively for its own glory. We should never forget this fundamental axiom. The finite must be, if I can put it this way, as radically finite as possible, as mediocre as possible, if we want its infinite redemption to be glorious, if we want the incorporation of the divine infinity into that finite to attest to the glory of God. In other words, the larger the gap to be bridged between finite and infinite, the more the infinite attests to its own glory in the finite, that is, in the other. Consequently, the world must be on the edge of nothingness, on the extreme edge of the nothing, and even as finite, within its very finitude, it must reveal its quasi-nothingness, in order for the Redemption by way of the Incarnation to be worthy of the glory of God. God's plan cannot be a finite perfection, i.e., a world. . . . We come back to the idea that, ultimately, the work matters little in comparison with the gesture. Finite perfection is an opportunistic thesis. In fact, God's plan is all the more admirable if the world is a quasi-nothingness. It should be understood that the problem, which will attest to God's glory, lies in the fact that God will incarnate himself in this quasi-nothingness. What counts is to manage to ensure that it is in this quasi-nothingness—in this absolute "on the edge of the nothing" that the world is—that God reveals and incarnates himself. It is, moreover, for this reason that the symbol will be the cross, the humiliated God, the suffering God, subjected to the horror of the world. The glory of God will be all the more obvious to the extent that God will descend not into a world that works relatively well, but into a horrible world, where he will be subjected to horror and mediocrity, to the nothingness of this world. God observes the Fall impassively, although the Fall is partly freely chosen and not entirely the result of calculation. But he has no reason to intervene to inhibit, interrupt, or limit the disaster, Adam's sin, the reign of injustice, because all of that is humanity's and the world's race to nothingness. Adam decided that the world was to be unjust, bloody, and terrible. But this is in no way incompatible with God's plan; on the contrary, it reinforces it. The farther the race into the nothing goes, the more the world will be on the edge of the void, and the more the Incarnation will testify to divine greatness and the glory of God. And Malebranche says so admirably. Speaking of God, he writes: "Remaining unmoved even as his Work is about to perish, he upholds with dignity the nature of the divinity in this way, and declares by his conduct that he is infinite and that the future Church sanctified in Jesus Christ is his true plan."[11] If God, by a particular will, had attempted to interrupt the fatal consequences of the Fall and of Adam's sin—which of course he could have—he would have purely and simply deviated from his plan and therefore from his essence. It is in this race to the nothing of this world that the conditions of maximal possibility of divine glorification, self-glorification, are inscribed. That's the first point.

The second point concerns, this time, the immanent, eternal operation that produces the Son as God, that produces Christ, an operator of God. The constant engendering of the Son is the engendering by God of his capacity to join with the finite, to incarnate himself. This is a relatively subtle point, grafted onto differences of causality. The engendering of the Son by the Father is not the creation of the finite itself, even though the Son is finite; it is the engendering of God's capacity to join with the finite. This is what I call an operator of God, a particular operator that makes him capable of joining with the finite. This capacity requires the nothingness of the world in order to function, because if the world were just, this operator would be devoid of sense and ultimately the sense of this operator is God's capacity for nothingness, a capacity that will be symbolized in Christianity by his death on the cross. The finite is nothingness. Christ is therefore this operator internal to being owing to which being becomes capable of nothingness. And it is the nothingness of the world, not its plenitude or relative perfection, that calls forth its use. Concerning the fact that God has impassively left the world in sin and let the Fall happen, Malebranche writes: "God did this so that his Son should have the glory of forming his Church from the nothingness of holiness and justice."[12] The Church is to be formed by Christ, the operator of God, out of the nothingness of justice and holiness, which fashions its glory. Therefore, in fact, what is at stake in this affair, and through which Malebranche corrects the perspectives after having radicalized them, is that the Christ-operator, as the ontological operator, has essentially nothing to do with sin and salvation; it has to do with being and nothingness. It is an ontological operator before being an eschatological one. In other words, the nothing is the maximal mediation of being in terms of taking leave of itself.

Next time we shall see, as we continue with this issue, that what we have here is an elucidation of the word "glory." Glory is what being derives from the Other, with a capital O. "Glory" connotes what, in being, derives from the nothing, because the Other of being, the place of the Other for being, is the nothing. Glory is therefore what being derives from the nothing. This is a very fitting definition of glory, and, to tell the truth, still very Cornelian. I will show that beneath its seemingly "noble" psychology, the concept of glory, too, is an ontological concept. We will study the consequences of all this for the fall/redemption couple as an operator of glory. And we will turn next to the question of the law, of the paradoxes of the law.

Session 4

April 15, 1986

I have already suggested that, for Malebranche, desire—even if this is not the word he uses—is a concept intrinsic to the examination of being. It is impossible to think the "what is," the "there is"—whether it's the "there is" of God or the "there is" of the world—without a host of categories, which are categories of subjectivity in general. That is moreover why, already during his lifetime, Malebranche was often criticized for being someone who put himself in God's place, whose philosophy in some sense installed itself in divine interiority. He was suspected of using an identification with God himself. In a way, this amounted to criticizing him for de-radicalizing divine transcendence, for not thinking it as radical alterity.

There are several reasons for this, if only because the formula "we see in God" can be taken in two senses. We see the visible in God is the first sense, and the second is: God is visible, we see clearly in God, meaning that his plans, far from being inscrutable, are on the contrary transparent. But more interesting and more essential than this ambiguity is the fact that the categories of the thinking of being are subjective categories—and that, for example, to think the world in its being and in the sense of its being, and to think God's plan for it, are one and the same thing. That's why, however you look at it, this is indeed a subjective ontology, in terms of both its destination and its categories.

The second point, which I've already mentioned but which needs to be stressed, is that we are dealing with an aesthetic ontology. The thinking of being is an aesthetics of the gesture, in this case of the divine gesture, which is intrinsic and thus part of the thinking of being. It mobilizes the old category of perfection, according to which God is the whole of all thinkable perfections. It is clear that Malebranche's deep conviction is that what exists can only be legitimized in terms of perfection. The fact that there is something rather than nothing—an old theological question—is thinkable for him only because that something has an intrinsic value, which gives it a superiority over nothing. Except that he won't settle for the old doctrine that, since it is more perfect than non-being, being qua being is in any event preferable, or superior, to nothing.

This is moreover a position Malebranche shared with Leibniz, which clearly shows that it was a thinking of the period. In the late seventeenth century people did not necessarily think it was self-evident that being was preferable to non-being. Being had to have a little something extra for it to be really accepted that there was something rather than nothing. Leibniz's response to the explicit question: "Why is there something rather than nothing?" was that "nothing" is easier than "something." This was a way of answering the same question from a different angle, namely by denouncing facility. Taking things in their ontological nakedness, you might think that, in a certain sense, it would be more reasonable for there to be nothing rather than something, because if you want to think something rather than nothing, you have to think more than just being, you have to think being's value: the "there is" is intrinsically valorizable, and not simply as "there is something." What Leibniz and Malebranche therefore had in common was that they had to prove, so to speak, that the world was beautiful, that being was beautiful, and they had to be able to base the superiority of something over nothing on a value. In Leibniz this value would be largely mathematical and aesthetic, but ultimately it would be moral—that is, the world would exist because it was the best possible world. For Malebranche, it was more explicitly aesthetic: there is something because the act that causes there to be something is, as a creative act, an ineffable beauty, a perfection. We have seen that for him "perfection" is understood in the sense of action rather than result. Which is quite profound: if there is something rather than nothing, it is because it was beautiful to create. Beauty lies essentially in the gesture that creates being and not just in its created objectivity. Consequently, creation is beautiful, and the creative gesture is the center of gravity of the evaluation.

From this point of view, perfection is the ways in which being is generously distributed. So we are dealing, in large part, with an artist God, a Baroque artist God, an artist God of the age. For how is this beauty of the gesture, this aesthetics of the prodigality of being, presented? It is presented according to the principle of the simplicity of ways. The world is justifiable because it results from a causality consistent with the great architectonic principle of producing the maximum effect with the minimum means. Thus: decorative luxuriance, ornamental multiplicity, the inexhaustible variety of the world of course, but on a legal basis, or on absolutely minimal principles. Therefore: minimal architecture and maximal ornamentation.

In this regard, what Leibniz and Malebranche had in common was a mathematical reference, which was the means, available at the time, for calculating the maxima and minima of functions. Since people were beginning to know what "speaking rationally" of the maximum and the minimum of a function meant, they could say: creation is a divine function, and the world must coincide with a maximum of this function. This mathematical reference was absolutely active and operative at the time, and it was a sort of common basis for both philosophers' thinking.

But clearly, whereas Leibniz privileged the mathematical or physical aspect of this reference, Malebranche aestheticized it, because he was much more overtly a theologian and a great deal more focused on the importance of the Christian notion of the subject. This was why his vision of being, a vision of being that was a vision in God, was an aesthetic pleasure afforded not so much by the world as by the act that creates it. The world is justified by an aesthetic pleasure. And what is remarkable is that this aesthetic pleasure acts as proof. This is why I spoke of an aesthetic ontology as regards Malebranche. That things are consistent with the principle of the maximum effect obtained by the minimum means acts as proof that the doctrine presented is correct. This is a very strange approach. It is not strictly speaking a deductive or demonstrative legitimation; it is, we might say, an aesthetic proof. According to Malebranche, for being to be legitimate it must be beautiful. And its aesthetic demonstration is operational and works. But it also works in the opposite direction: the fact that it is beautiful proves that being is. Beauty also acts as the proof of being.

We will see later on how this works for the doctrine of grace, because there is also an aesthetics of grace, an aesthetics of salvation—and, ultimately, you are saved provided you fully participate in the beauty of the world, that is, provided you are not a quirky, out-of-place ornament, something that spoils or clashes with the aesthetic pleasure. In a sense, according to the principles of this aesthetics, you're doomed if you're ugly inasmuch as (since beauty is a predicate of being) ugliness is non-being. We are obviously coming back here to the major currents of thought that represent sin as a nothingness. But here the real figure of nothingness is ugliness; sin is ugliness. The metaphor of the soul's ugliness, of sin as the soul's ugliness, is ancient, but Malebranche takes it literally, in its effective aesthetic meaning.

As far as method is concerned, two points must now be emphasized, which I will summarize in broad strokes. First, the dependence on a single axiom. To have a single axiom is to act like God: maximum effect with minimum means. If you can derive pretty much all your philosophical considerations from a single axiom, you are doing philosophy according to the principle of the simplicity of ways. Malebranche's philosophy is constructed in conformity with God's plan for constructing the world. This is very evident in his writing, which is fluid and supple: to speak of an identification, in this case, is not totally off the mark. It is a matter of being in a relationship with the system's architectonicity that is analogous to divine creation insofar as he'll seek the smallest possible number of principles, from which he'll derive the largest possible number of results. This is also what explains the Baroque appearance of Malebranche's philosophy, which consists of a simple structure overloaded with additions, ornaments, digressions, summaries, etc. The work's style reflects God's style. This is entirely natural, since this philosophical truth is itself seen in God: because this God is an artist God, the art of the thought also reflects God's aesthetic principle. The first consequence to be derived from this single axiom—which, may I remind you, is that God can only act for his own glory—is that glory is the relation of finality of the infinite with itself. But the infinite can only will itself since it lacks nothing.

A brief digression is in order here. This is a very interesting issue, because Malebranche's big problem will be how to think desire without lack. Glory, as we shall see, is ultimately a category of God's desire: what God desires is his own glory. This goes without saying, because if he didn't desire it, he wouldn't make anything, and especially not the world. So he has to desire something. Except that it would be completely heretical to suggest that God lacked something.

God is obviously supreme perfection, completeness, self-sufficient totality. Where could a lack be introduced into him? Nevertheless, Malebranche wants to think that God desires. What is more, desiring oneself and not desiring are two completely different things. So he'll have to think how, subjectively, there can be desire without lack. Remember that the world results from this desire because, if you say that the world is the result of the fact that "God desires his own glory," it is because this desire is productive. Something therefore happened: there was a divine act or, as Malebranche will say, God went outside himself, went outside himself in order to posit a finite world. There had to have been desire for this action to occur, but in the case of God, that desire must not mean that a lack will be filled. Certainly the world, for its part, will lack everything if it is finite, but this is not connected to God, who is supreme infinity, and therefore lacks nothing.

Whether there can be a conceivable thinking of desire that is free from all thinking of lack is a major, very interesting problem for us. Lack is many things, but it is in any event a category of the symbolic, a fundamental category of the law. A law is always what regulates lack or deficiency. We can therefore ask whether there can be a possible thinking of desire without the law. And we are forced to respond "no." Things become complicated for Malebranche, because if there is no lack, there can be no other-than-God, something God would lack; there can be no symbolic horizon for God's desires. What is more, this other would be an other of the Other, for naturally the absolute Other is God himself. As there can be no other of the Other, there can be no law for God. But then, where does God's desire come from? Because we know very well that, to use Lacan's terminology, desire is reciprocal to the law. On that note I'll end this digression, which was a brief look ahead to a further discussion of the issue later on. But you can see the crux of the question Malebranche is circling around. It's a focal point for his entire doctrine.

So much for the dependence on a single axiom. The second methodological point I highlighted was the use of balancing mediations. There, too, Malebranche proceeds in aesthetic terms, through tensions that are resolved usually thanks to the introduction of a third term. But once more, what is profoundly Baroque about his work is that when he examines a third term or a tension, he always begins by compounding the problem he wants to solve. He is not someone who tries to reduce the tensions, the bipolarities, or the contradictions; to the contrary, he stretches them to their limit so that the balancing solution will be virtuosic. For the more you stretch things, the more the intervention of the third, balancing term will be surprising and appear as a tour de force. There is clearly a sense of philosophical virtuosity about Malebranche that is oddly enough not a deductive or abstract virtuosity but a virtuosity of balances and counterbalances. He is an acrobat of the concept. It's very clear that he is sure that this is the way he'll best succeed in being convincing. After all, the balancing mediation might work, or it might not . . . But he expects from the virtuoso effect an effect of persuasion: if you truly surprise the reader by restoring a balance that seemed completely destroyed, the reader will be pleased—aesthetically pleased—and therefore convinced. Here again, the search for aesthetic pleasure is a law of the text, not just a law of the world.

I've examined this approach with regard to a first major problem, the one that has to do with Christ's, hence the Redeemer's, relationship to the Fall. If God created the world only for his own glory, hence in order for there to be Christ—that is, in order for there to be the Church—how can we avoid the idea that he also willed the Fall, and therefore sin? Once the Redeemer has come down to earth to redeem men's sins, assuming that the objective was for him to come down there, this would mean that sin involves profit and loss. We are on the verge of the doctrine that says God, always for his own glory, would explicitly will evil. We have seen that Malebranche begins by compounding the problem as much as possible. He will say: it is not true that evil is purely negative; evil exists, truly, it is positive. Insofar as he refuses every intermediary solution, he will give what is in my opinion a trompe l'oeil—as befits Baroque art—solution, a very farfetched but very satisfying one, namely that if being goes outside itself, if God goes outside himself, the maximal mediation of this self-externalization is obviously nothingness. Consequently, the more null the world is—that is to say, minimal in its being—or the more finite it is, the more the descent of the infinite into this finiteness glorifies divine capacity. The maximum of glory—here we find the simplicity of ways again—is obtained paradoxically by a minimum of world since glory is the capacity of the infinite to descend into the finitude of the world. Therefore, the closer the world is to the brink of nothingness, to the brink of the void, the more glorious this descent of the infinity of being into the world is. No objection here: the principle requires that the world be minimal, because it is with a minimal world that the simple action of the incarnation of God, therefore of Christ, obtains the maximum effect, this effect being glory for God.

The logic is quite clear: maximum glory is obtained provided there is a minimum of world. But this minimum of world is the addition of two things: its finitude and its nothingness. The world must be minimum in terms of nature—we know that it is finite—but also minimum in terms of the spirit. Now, what plunges the spirit into nothingness is precisely sin, the corruption of the soul. God did not will sin; God willed his glory. But insofar as willing his glory obeys, like everything, the principle of the simplicity of ways, and insofar as the maximum of glory can therefore only be obtained through a minimum of world—a quantitative minimum (the world is finite) and a qualitative minimum (the spirit is sinful)—the world had to be humiliated, including spiritually. Therefore, it had to contain

corruption and sin, so that the coming of God into this humiliated, nullified, minimalized world might be maximally glorious.
This is moreover why God himself plunged into the depths of this
humiliation. He was tortured, crucified, and insulted, he was intimately acquainted with this nothingness of the world—the result of
which was his most extreme glorification.

It could be objected that it would have been enough to say that God
wills only his glory. But it must be understood that, in this case, the
way God willed his glory was to create a world. However, this world
is evil, and in order to set it aright, a Redeemer was necessary. As
a result, the correlation initially appears as a correlation between
Fall and Redemption, and we run the risk of thinking that it is this
very correlation that God willed. This is why the demonstration
amounts to saying that the ultimate correlation is not between
Christ and the Fall, which is only a side effect for which God is not
directly responsible. The founding correlation is the one between
Christ and glory, and which, when confronted with the principle
of the simplicity of ways, obtains the maximum of glory with the
most abject of worlds. This explains why this world is the most
abject world possible, both materially (it is wretched) and spiritually (it is humiliated).

So this is what leads me to follow up with a reconsideration of
the question of glory. In the case we are dealing with, i.e., glory
insofar as it involves the creation of the world and the descent
of Christ into this humiliated world (thereby producing a maximal glory with principles that are as minimal as possible), what is
striking is that glory is partly what being derives from the other.
Indeed, the created world is other than God—radically other, since
it is finite, and finitude is truly what is other than God, since God
is infinite. It follows necessarily that, since God is being, what is
other than being is ultimately nothingness. Consequently, if glory

involves the other, which is the case, this glory is necessarily all the greater the more other this other is. Therefore, glory will be all the more glorious the more null this other is. In conclusion—this is the logic of glory—the world must be as nil as possible. And yet, nothingness is impossible because if there is one thing God cannot do, it is to choose nothingness. We are on a very fine line here between "as null as possible," which is required for glory, and the "not entirely nothing." Whence Malebranche's constant tendency to nullify the world as much as possible—to the point where it was sometimes said that Malebranche's otherness was not really an otherness, and he was accused of Spinozism because of his systematic determination to nullify the world.

Indeed, with every problem he treats, be it sensible perception or causality, there is a constant struggle against the being of the world, i.e., against its autonomy insofar as the world is in God, purely and simply. He will say: there is no causality in the world, since it is in God; or, I do not see the sensible directly, I see it in God, etc. In Malebranche the world is always almost an illusion: as soon as any determination is accorded it, he is suspicious of it and de-realizes it, or refers it to God. The deep logic at work is clear: since the other-than-God is nothingness, and if glory depends on the other, the world must be as minimal as possible. Malebranche must work his way toward a minimality of the world, toward its quasi-nothingness. Here again is the calculating of maxima and minima. There must be a minimum, because if there is no minimum at all, there can be no glorious self-externalization. Whence the fine line. If you put in too much world, you are too far from nothingness, thus too far from the radical alterity with respect to God. But if you don't put in enough world, there is no longer any world at all, hence no process either. This whole approach leads Malebranche to a particular doctrine of what, today, with Lacan and some others, we might call the real. He touches this real because, finally, he would like the world to be a pure "there is," with no density at all: a tiny point, a pure point of being.

Note the ambiguity of the term *point d'être*: "pure point of being," which also means "no being at all." This is typical Malebranche. It could sum him up. A good deal of his critical analysis on this issue is very subtle. With the fine line that passes between "minimum of being" and "nothing at all," he gives us a sort of occulted real, or a ghostly—elusive but at the same time absolutely irreducible—"pure point of being/no being at all": the world, as compared with its Creator, is absolutely nothing, and yet it is the other-than-God, an irreducible otherness. The world is the other-than-being, but apart from that, it is nothing. It is what I called a pure "there is." God ensures his glory only to the extent that he descends into such a pure point of being/no being at all. The doctrine of the Incarnation, the suffering body of Christ, the blood, the spear: it is clear that for Malebranche these are only metaphors; there is far too much being in them. On closer inspection, in any case, these aren't things that can be perceived. The Incarnation is not an actualization of God; I would say instead that it is a "real-ization," that is, God's becoming the real, pure point of being/no being at all. But it is when he is real that God is in his glory. "Real," but we must see in what sense: not the real of luminous majesty, but on the contrary the real of eclipse, the real of the pure point of being/no being at all, the real of the quasi-nothing. As a result, the connection here between Christ and God, between the two persons of the Father and the Son, is a relation in which, instead of the null density in which the other is situated, the father has the son as his real point.

I come now to the second major problem. The first was the question of Christ and the Fall. The second—which actually stems from everything I just explained—is the following: if God can act only by general will, if he can only act according to the principle of the simplicity of ways, is he not subject to a necessity? Isn't there an other of the Other, namely, the principles of the divine aesthetic? If we agree that God is a Baroque artist, there are necessarily rules for his art. But what, then, is the status of these rules? If divine action is forced to comply with this or that principle, isn't there a necessity that is transcendent to God himself? Since God in his action, in his gesture, is compelled to submit to it, isn't a principle such as the simplicity of ways ultimately beyond God himself? This is a big problem, and of course it was objected to Malebranche that he subjected God to an external necessity and made a mockery of divine freedom.

As usual, Malebranche will begin by seriously compounding the problem. To begin with, he will say that God never changes his mind, which is a constraint. Whatever the effects of his undertakings, God never revisits them, even if the effects are horrifying. He writes: "God never regrets or never changes plans."[1] This is a thesis of indifference to effects. The sight of the effects, including potentially mechanical ones, of what God commands leaves him indifferent. And we can moreover see from this that this is not exactly the God of the Old Testament, who was quite capable of changing plans. Malebranche ends up coming right out and saying that God has a weakness: "It is not in God's power to go back on himself or to have scorn for the laws his own wisdom prescribes for him." Note that the term "law" appears in two modes: God prescribes the law to himself, obviously, but once he has prescribed it, he can no longer change it. Consequently, and this is a very important point, God has no capacity for transgression. If we compare the two formulas, we see, on the one hand, that God cannot change his action in midstream—which means that any of God's gestures is unique and cannot be broken down into contradictory sequences—and, on the other hand, that God has no transgressive capacity with regard to the law. This is indeed a considerable accumulation of problems, since not only is there the law but, as regards the law, there are at the same time an impassibility and indifference to the effects of the law, and an inability to transgress it.

The second way Malebranche compounds problems leads back to the question of evil. We saw that evil was induced by divine action—whose ultimate purpose is the glory of God—and therefore by the laws of action and the aesthetics of the glorious gesture. But God might have been able to renounce his glory. Of course, the axiom says "God acts only for his own glory," but nothing prevents his renouncing this glory that comes at such a high price, a price he, in his omniscience, knows. Once God has acted, there is evil. He is certainly not responsible for it, but he knows it exists. Therefore, he is at least responsible for the fact that he could have not acted. Given the vast number of eternal torments, of souls lost because they were ugly, it's really quite a heavy price to pay. So we could imagine that, to eliminate the problem, Malebranche would say, no, God necessarily had to act and could only will his own glory, etc. But that's not what he says. He even explicitly says: "[God] can not act." And he adds: "He is quite indifferent in this matter, for he suffices completely to himself."[2] This, then, will lead us into problems of the utmost interest to us.

Let's assess the real importance of this second way of compounding problems. Not acting, and therefore not going outside himself, no world at all: all of this was possible. All the more possible insofar as God is fully sufficient unto himself. Therefore, God had no need of an other. So why did he act? We will be told: he acted for his glory. But this answer does not eliminate the problem. On the one hand, when God acts, he acts for his own glory, but he can also not act, since he is fully sufficient unto himself. The subtlety of the problem is as follows: glory is the principle of divine action, but it is not the principle of the existence of this action. In other words, if the world is created, it is for God's own glory. But the fact that the world is created raises a question that the concept of glory does not entirely satisfy. We should not confuse the principle of an action with the principle of the being of this action. These are two distinct things. And all the more distinct insofar as God, once again, could easily have not acted. The difference is very interesting, because it is true that we often think we have interpreted an action sufficiently when we have discovered its meaning. Now, if we take the creation of the world as an action, its meaning is the glory of God, and consequently Christ, the cross, and so on. Sure. But there is something in the action other than its meaning: there is its existence, there is the real act, and nothing tells us that the existence of an action is intrinsically exhausted by its meaning when the possibility of not acting exists.

We must therefore introduce something other than the fact that God works for his own glory, and this something else can only be a desire. Desire is different from a principle. The meaning of the action can involve a principle, but the being of the action involves a desire. We must therefore think this: God has the desire to be God. Necessarily, for otherwise it would be impossible to understand why he would have created the world. The fact that God has the desire to be God justifies not the meaning of the world but its being: it is in fact the "there is" of the "there is." It could be put differently: if God did not act, he would not be a subject. Of course, he is fully sufficient unto himself, but he would not be a subject. It is certain, then, that being as subject, as Malebranche understands it, requires that God desire to be God. In other words, being is the desire to be.

In the final analysis, what does "God desires to be God" mean, since he in fact *is* God? We won't be there for the genesis of God: God is God. The desire to be God is the only conceivable desire for him. It is worth noting that, ultimately, this desire to be God will be fulfilled by being a man, through Christ. We have not yet seen the figures of perversion adequate to this desire. But we should first of all go the root of the problem and ask: what can the desire to be God possibly mean for God? Well, it can't be the desire to be God as being, because God as being is the support of desire, and, as I said, God cannot desire to become God. It is therefore necessarily the desire that being God should have a meaning, and therefore the desire of God as meaning and not as being. To say: God desires to be God is in fact to say: God desires to produce this meaning that is God. And producing this meaning that is God will necessarily unfold in the logic of glory. But the logic of glory will be the principle of divine action, not its being. Its being is justifiable only through God's desire to be God as meaning. That's practically pre-Hegelian. God will want to go outside himself so as to get away from the stupidity of being, so as to come about as meaning—that is, so that there might be a meaning to being God. Hegel, for his part, would say: the infinite is meaningful only if there is the finite. Such is the dialectical vision of the matter: in order for the infinite to acquire its own meaning, there must necessarily be the finite. In Malebranche, things are bit more convoluted: God will come about as meaning—indeed, there will be a being of his action—but the only possible meaning of being-God is for him to desire his own glory. In fact, God desires for God to have a meaning. There is no possible meaning that can be assigned to God other than the fact of acting in accordance with his own glory, or for his own glory. God therefore desires for God to will his own glory, because God is desire for his meaning. God desires to stage the question of his glory. This is what will lead him to create the world, it being understood that, in creating the world, he strictly obeys the logic of glory. But in reality, the world—that is, this "other" place—will be the scene of God's desire as production of a meaning, which is glory. So it is necessary to say explicitly that the world is God's fantasy.

In Malebranche this is extremely rigorous and there is precisely the matheme of the fantasy, in the Lacanian sense. Indeed, what is the world? The world, as I said a moment ago, is an occulted object, a "there is" on the brink of the void, a flickering "quasi-nothing," hence truly Lacan's famous *objet a*, the object that is the cause of desire. An object for what subject? For the subject of the desire that is God, which is obviously irreducibly split, split between Father and Son. Therefore, on the level of desire—what I am calling desire here, and what Malebranche calls God's ultimate plans—there is the world as God's fantasy: the correlation between a quasi-null object and a subject divided into Father and Son, a split subject, thereby constituting a *scene*: a word which, incidentally (let's take advantage of the ambiguity [in French]), could be written with a "c", "*cène*" [the Last Supper], where a meaning comes into being for God, his meaning, a meaning that is his own glory.

But it's not over, because this correlation—which is a desiring one this time—between God and the world requires as a third position a fixed symbolic order, namely, the one I mentioned: the principle of the simplicity of ways. As Malebranche says: "Order is God's inviolable law."[3] Naturally, principles come from God. And what should be stressed is that, right from the beginning, God designates the reciprocity of law and desire. "Law" and "desire" are the two names whose site is God. He is originally law and desire. Faithful to classical theology, Malebranche says quite simply: God is wisdom and power, or wisdom and will. As wisdom, he is law; as will, he is desire, in the sense I mentioned. Naturally, if he can be desire it is solely because there is law. And Malebranche is acutely aware of this. In the process, he gets rid of the objection that God would be subject to the law as to something external and transcendent. God is in no way subject to the law, given that this law is the condition of his desire. How could he desire to be God if there was no law? That would make no sense. In the absence of the law he would be in a state of self-sufficiency, of self-sufficient plenitude. If the Christian God is not in the plenitude of self-sufficiency, it is precisely because he is both law and desire. The law is not what prevents or prohibits him from desiring—what, outside him, would limit his very being—for his being is him, and consequently his being is reciprocal to the law. Nor would a being without law, a God without law—assuming such a thing is thinkable for Malebranche—be able to desire itself. All we could say about a God without law is that he is. He could certainly not be the Christian God, for nothing of what has been said about the creation of the world or Christ, etc., would be intelligible, because we wouldn't be able to think the being of creation. We might able to think its meaning, but not its being. We can only think the being of creation if we think God as desire. But to think God as desire, we must—it's one and the same thing—also think him as law. And the law is the aesthetic law of the simplicity of ways.

That is Malebranche's choice, the law of that day and age, we might say. But even assuming this law could be renounced, another one would in any case be necessary. We could easily imagine a Malebranchian system with a different aesthetic—a Malebranchian God with a contemporary aesthetic, for example. That's not the problem. In reality, the content of the law itself—the Baroque aesthetic of the prescription—is not the determining factor. The most important point is whether God can be thought as desire. It's clear that this is a requisite for Malebranche, because otherwise we could not understand why there is a world. So if we truly think the world as God's fantasy—and for Malebranche this is ultimately the only correct way to think it—we must also think the law. Otherwise, the system would be incomplete and begin to malfunction. The absolute rule, which is here the simplicity of ways, could easily be another rule. It's not a transcendent necessity but an immanent condition of being as subject—or, here, of God as desire.

The scene where all of this is situated is none other than the world. So it's a macroscopic image. Malebranche is a bit like that, giving us a macroscopic image of the subject. Some give us a microscopic image; he gives us a macroscopic one. It's not a "subject," it's "God." It's not an "object," it's the "world." It's not the "signifying law," it's the "simplicity of ways," in the sense of divine wisdom. This leads to the whole psychoanalytic system, and we have the right to ask what the doctrine of the neuroses and perversions of God might be. This is indeed the meaning of Lacan's famous formula: "God is unconscious."

It is nevertheless striking that God's desire, which can only be the desire to be God—that is, to produce God as meaning—should be fulfilled by a crucifixion. It is striking in a symptomatic way. But if we admit that the world is God's fantasy—let's not forget that the world, in Malebranche's sense, is the world with Christ, the world without Christ being the quasi-nothing—how is God depicted in this fantasy? As it happens, he is depicted in agony. This is an issue to explore, and I urge you to systematically seek out exactly what Malebranche says about it, that is, what the precise Malebranchian doctrine of the cross, of the symbol of the cross, is. You will realize by yourselves that he doesn't much care to speak about it, but it is interesting to see just how he does speak about it.

Another angle, which would require a substantial amount of analysis, is the following: there is the law and there is no transgressive capacity in God. Yet there are transgressions, the transgressions that miracles are. After all, Malebranche won't risk going to the stake by denying miracles! As I've said from the beginning, he's an orthodox. He must therefore also think miracles. However, the first description of miracles amounts to positing that they are a transgression of natural laws. Here again, we're confronted with a compounded problem, since God has no ability to transgress the law. Unlike other theologians for whom there is no established category of God's subjection to a legal order, in Malebranche this category is completely established. It is not simply established, but he explicitly says that in the case of the law there is neither any going back nor any exception. And yet: there are miracles, and so there are in fact exceptions. Here we're in an extreme state of tension, for which some balancing mediation must be found. How can the principle that God cannot transgress the law be maintained, while at the same time admitting that there are flagrant examples of just such a transgression? This requires a whole doctrine of balancing, which represents a new cycle of Malebranche's undertaking. That's what we'll venture into next time because in order to account for miracles, the law will have to be changed, at least apparently. In any case, the order will have to be changed. Basically, it will be necessary to switch from the order of nature to the order of grace. And—to take up the outline of the conceptual investigation again as a metaphor—I think we could say: the order of nature is the one in which can be discerned the perverse character of God's desire, which appears in the examination of finitude as such, of the quasi-nothing—that is, of God's staging of himself as an object, of God as an object. It is ultimately the staging of God himself in the form of Christ as quasi-nothing, which allows us—without excusing it!—to speak of a certain masochism in God. Who cannot see that all glory presupposes the acceptance of such a masochism? On the other hand, the order of grace is, as we will see, the order of God's neurosis. It would be very interesting to ask whether it's hysterical or obsessional, for a completely obvious reason directly related to the problem of grace in a descriptive way. Grace, apparently, is absolutely capricious; it falls we know not where, or why. This is the hysterical side of things. But, on the other hand, it also falls all of the time. It is therefore compulsive. This is the obsessional side. Grace is therefore something we can always count on—God goes to obsessive lengths to ensure that grace can always be counted on—but in another sense, it cannot be counted on at all. It is fleeting and arbitrary. This order of grace is controlled by the very curious concept of arbitrary repetition. This is why I spoke in this regard about a neurotic undecidability. It is this investigation of the order of grace that we will take up next time.

Session 5

April 29, 1986

Malebranche might be said to have had an acute awareness of the contradiction between the assumption that God is a subject and the assumption that he is perfect. Even though Malebranche doesn't formulate it in exactly those terms, it is in his eyes undoubtedly the central contradiction of a Christian ontology. There is a contradiction between the absolute self-sufficiency that perfection, infinite perfection, implies and the regime of action, the regime of intervention that the position as subject implies. This is why I proposed—in language that is not entirely Malebranche's but, as we'll soon see, is not so far off after all—the idea that, ultimately, what interests him is to think God as a desiring being, and thus to introduce *in fine* a radical split into his self-sufficiency. No matter how you approach the question—even without using the most sophisticated problematics of desire—it is clear that anyone who desires is not self-sufficient. So if you think God as a subject, you must think that God desires, and you're forced to undermine his self-sufficiency, or at any rate his self-sufficiency as plenitude, as full substantiality. I also stressed that what is crucial for Malebranche is that God desire to be God. It is not enough for him to be God, which is why he is not, strictly speaking, self-sufficient. Indeed, it is clear that if God desires to be God, this implies that his desire is situated in the place of the other. There must therefore be an ex-centering, a place of the other, where this desire to be God can be something other than being-God.

This question has two sides to it. The first is that God in no way created the world capriciously; he created the world so that there would be the place that is other than his desire to be God. This is really the meaning of Malebranche's formulation: "He created the world in order to establish his Church." For the Church is the temple of God's desire. Neither a capricious fulguration, nor an incomprehensible excess, the world was created by God because he is a desiring being, one that should be thought as a subject, which requires that there be the place that is other than his desire to be God. What Malebranche calls "glory" is precisely this complex structure, this divine desire to be God, linked to the need for there to be this place that is other for his desire. The other aspect of this problem—which I examined at great length—is the following: this other place where God can give form to his desire, or more precisely the object of his desire—i.e., himself, but in the form of something other than himself (that's why there's the Father and the Son)—is necessarily the place of nothingness, for being that fully is, is God. Therefore, the other-than-God is not-being.

And as a result, God can only be a subject through the mediation of nothingness. In Malebranche's eyes, this is what Christianity alone can think because, ultimately, at the heart of things, there is the death of God. But the death of God is really the *parousia* of his desire.

Let's recapitulate a number of things that I already said. If this other place of God's desire is essentially nothingness—that is, the pathetic finitude of the world (if it is nothing, absolutely nothing, as compared with divine plenitude)—we immediately see that we've got the structure of an object, an object on the verge of disappearing, an eclipsed object, an object on the brink of the void.

The object proper to God's desire is therefore to give form to him-self as a kind of vanishing, as nothingness, or in the position of an eclipsed object. Which is obviously—in truly non-Malebranchian terms—a phantasmal scene. The world, ultimately, is the scene of the divine fantasy.

Let's remember that this intelligible scheme of God as subject, hence of being as subject, this becoming-subject of being, as desire of self in the place of the other, requires the law. I in fact discussed the question of in what sense God is subject to a law. Malebranche has an acute—and, in my opinion, very modern—awareness of the fact that it is totally impossible to think desire without thinking the law. The reciprocal nature of desire and the law is a truly central theme for him. The divine will can only be understood—Malebranche speaks of the "divine will," but also, as we shall soon see, of "desire" as well—under condition of the law. This law is that God can act only by general will, and therefore that he always obeys the aesthetic principle of the simplicity of ways. That's the explicit content, but at a deep level it means the following, which is the crux of the question: the law, within the specific order I'm speaking about, codes the rela-tionship between being and nothingness, or between the infinite and the finite, or between God and the world—and therefore, finally, between the subject and the object. And so this law, to which the creation and the maintaining of the world are subject, creates, in relation to the pair infinite/finite or being/nothingness, what I would call an "intersecting" relation.

Let me explain. If we admit that the space of the law codes the relationship between being and nothingness or the infinite and the finite, we can see that being clearly has primacy and a radical supremacy over nothingness. But what happens with the law, which is governed by the simplicity of ways, the principle of maximum effects, etc.? What happens is that a maximum effect in terms of nothingness, hence in terms of the world, must be obtained with a minimum of principles in terms of being. That's the law, for God. Therefore, in ontological terms, maximality is on the side of being and minimality on the side of nothingness: God and the world, the infinite and the finite, and so on. The principle of the maximum is on the side of the (worldly, finite, natural) effects; the principle of economy or minimality is on the side of the cause, on God's side, on the side of being, on the side of supremacy. God must, as it were, save being (his wisdom, the principles, intelligibility) in order to enrich nothingness, that is, in order to produce the maximum number of effects in the world. And so, in a certain sense, the law goes against the grain of the disproportion between the infinite and the finite. Underlying all of this, there is something completely remarkable in this figure of the law: a sacrifice for the sake of the object. God submits to the law so that the object can shine all the more brightly, so that it can be beautiful, in the sense of the Baroque beauty of the world—such is Malebranche's aesthetic—of the ornamental beauty of the world. And in order for this object to shine, for it to be infinitely multiple, ornamented, and full of spectacular effects, the being that creates it must be economized, must be subject to a nonprodigality, to as few principles as possible. Whereas, quite obviously, God could, through a particular decision, give form to whatever he wanted. This can only be understood if we put it back into the general architecture I spoke about. But it is indeed a matter of law. In more ontological terms, it could be said, in this connection, that the law links being to nothingness, codes the relationship between being and nothingness, since it determines a certain limitation of being in order to make nothingness be, so that the world can bountifully dispense its finitude. Ultimately, God must be skeletally one so that the world can be prodigiously multiple. Because it is, in fact, the world that seduces God, the world that is, ultimately, the scene of his desire. The world is God's fetish. That's why it has to be heavily ornamented. And compared with this worldly ornamentation, the subject, on the other hand, must present itself as empty, as a mere *mark*, or as skeletally subject to the law.

Finally, as the last point of this overview, the relation to nothingness, the relation to the world, splits the subject, splits God. In effect, the subject can maintain its relation to the object-world only as divided, and we have seen that the duality of persons, Father/Son, names this division. God's desire is dictated by his coming about as himself in the place of the other, and therefore by his transmuting his being into nothingness. Once more, what God desires is to be God. Now, all of this machinery controls the fact that he can only desire to be God insofar as God himself is nothingness, or in any case can become nothingness: can die, can be in the world, can stand on the phantasmal stage of the world. You'll note that the cleavage between Father and Son is truly a subjective cleavage; it is a nonsubstantial cleavage. It is an evasive "two," as the Church Fathers, those great men of science, were long ago careful to state: the distinction between persons is not substantial, but rather internal to a substantial unicity. At bottom, what Malebranche implicitly maintains is that this duality, which is not a duality in being—there are not two gods, the Father and the Son; there is only one—is only really intelligible for a God as subject. It is in effect difficult to think that the transcendent God, in his being, is two. Everything becomes clearer if we think God as subject, because what we encounter that way is the cleavage itself. The cleavage with regard to the object. Malebranche's stroke of genius was to think that this object—this evanescent object, this ever-lost object, always on the edge of the void, but at the same time adorned with all the attributes of beauty—that this object is the world, and that that's what divides God.

Since God is not so much God as the fact that he desires to be God, and since, on top of that, he is divided by the object that is the cause of his desire, what is God as being, ultimately? God as being would have to be thought through the retroaction of his division: God is what supports the schism; he is the Father and the Son. In the retroaction of this schism, God is truly void, and if you try to think God outside the set of operations I've just referred to—creation of the world, staging of the desire, will to glory, etc.—you find something that, in Malebranche's own eyes, does not exist, namely, the self-sufficiency of this God, this transcendent and self-sufficient God, who is in fact unintelligible. In the retroaction of his division, God is empty: he is only his process, only his action.

Here, a brief remark about the hypotheses I mentioned is in order. I said that, under the name "glory," that enigma of glory, we must think that God desires to be God, and that glory cannot be thought as an extra term, a quality that would be a supplement. Glory is fundamentally what God desires: namely, to be God. But in fact, it could be argued that, more radically, what God desires is to desire. Naturally, insofar as he desires, he can only desire to be God.

That goes without saying, since he is under the regime of solitary infinity. But I would maintain that what all of this machinery stages is in reality the desire of desire, the desire to be a subject, thus the desire not to just be being. The complex machinery of the world, of Christ's redemption, of the Church, etc.—all of it under the name of glory—is the basis for there being both God's desire and for being to be subjective. But there is an absolutely striking circularity to this in Malebranche. The world proves to us that God is a subject, for there is no reason for the finite except for the hypothesis that there is God. But the hypothesis that there is God is essentially the original ontological thesis. For Malebranche, as for Christian ontology, the fact that there is God is the same thing as solving the problem of why there is something rather than nothing. He won't do away with this originary ontological thesis just like that.

The world, for its part, proves something else to us. It doesn't prove that there is God. That is the Aristotelian and the Thomist approach.

The world proves to us that God is a subject, which is something different. The world is ultimately in the position of an object vis-à-vis God's desire. But the whole point is to determine what proves to us that there is a world. The world clearly proves that God desires, but what proves to us that there is a world? I already spoke to you about that very interesting sort of balancing. Traditionally, the world is certain and God is problematic. So proving God on the basis of the world was the approach of medieval—or even, in some respects, Cartesian—rationalism. Once more, paradoxically, Malebranche turns the problem around: for him, God is certain and the world is problematic. As we've seen, his approach involves trying to give a status to the world on the basis of God, a status that is moreover quite complicated. Indeed, what proves to us that there is a world? Malebranche's answer is categorical: nothing. Nothing, except for one thing. The only thing that proves to us that there is a world is Revelation, Scripture, God. Not in the sense where there would be a rational induction of God from the world, but of the world from God because he said as much. When we read Scripture, we are forced to think that there is a world.

God's fantasy exists because God told us about it. It is he who said, "My desire has an object." Otherwise, we wouldn't know about it. And so the certainty of the existence of the world has the status of a secret confided to us, God's secret, almost an erotic one: God told us about his fantasy, he confided it to us, because that's part of his fantasy. He needs to confide to us that the world exists, needs us to know that we are the object of his desire. Not because he wants to tell us the truth, or because he's honest, but because his desire needs him to do so. Whence—and this is very important—the secret he confides to us through the sacred texts. Naturally, we recognize here the structure of the contract, where it said and stated that so-and-so is the object of desire. It is up to this one whether to accept this status or not. Malebranche says this, not exactly in this

language, but almost in these very terms. Let's take the Fall. The ago-
nizing question of the Fall, along with original sin: men have sinned
and they are therefore truly in nothingness, and God presumably
willed all this! The objection returns time and again. I told you how
Malebranche got around it in its general sense. But it comes back to
Malebranche all the time in the following form: according to your
system, God truly desired man's fall, he knew about it, he planned
it, and it's really an abominable act. One of Malebranche's responses
is to say that accepting sin and man's fall allows God to declare what
his plan is. As you can see, I didn't make up this idea of a declaration, of God's confiding to us the structure of being of his desire.
By this declaration God at least said what he wanted of us. Had
he kept us in Eden, he would not have said what he wanted, what
he desired; namely, glory in the place of the other, in the place of
nothingness. By so doing, he showed himself to be true. Otherwise,
he would have hidden the truth, which would have been unworthy
of his greatness and his wisdom. He would have been shy; someone
who doesn't speak is shy. But here there's no shyness. Everyone falls,
but at least his desire was declared. And we know where we stand.
Otherwise, we would not be able to know what God wants of us, nor
even, as a result, why we exist. Through the Fall, we truly learn the
status of our existence, namely that we are objects of God's desire—
which, had our Adamic status been maintained, we would still know
nothing about.

In order to recapitulate all of these themes, I would now like to
read you a very striking text by Malebranche. It's at the very beginning of the second part of the First Discourse, in article 24:

> God, loving himself by the necessity of his being, and wanting to
> procure for himself an infinite glory, an honour perfectly worthy of
> himself, consults his wisdom concerning the accomplishment of his
> desires. This divine wisdom, filled with love for him from whom it

receives its being through an eternal and ineffable generation, seeing nothing in all possible creatures (whose intelligible ideas it contains) that is worthy of the majesty of its Father, offers itself to establish an eternal cult in his honour and as sovereign priest, to offer him a victim who, by the dignity of his person, is capable of contenting him.[1]

You can see that, in this text, we find what I said in almost the same terms. But what's interesting is the status of the word "wisdom." God wants to procure for himself an infinite glory that would be truly worthy of himself: he wants to be glorious, wants to be truly God, and so he consults his wisdom. This wisdom considers the possible objects and, not finding any that can really be the cause of God's desire, it decides to offer itself up as a victim worthy of God. A victim thanks to whom an eternal cult in honor of God will be established, a victim who will be capable of contenting him. What is this wisdom that is consulted here? It is in fact an attribute of God himself. It is what prescribes and determines the object of God's desire. Wisdom is therefore the structure of desire. And so every time Malebranche speaks of wisdom, or consults it concerning his desire, "wisdom" must be understood as referring to the structured nature of God's desire, as that through which his cause and therefore his object takes shape. In this particular case, Christ is naturally the victim worthy of God, and, of course, God himself. The only victim who is capable of contenting God's desire is obviously God himself, inasmuch as God is able to present himself in the figure of nothingness. And so we can say that Christ is a wise production of desire; he is structured desire. As you can see, the words "desire" and "contenting" (and so on) are explicitly present in Malebranche's text. So we see the extent to which God himself is situated in the subjective attribution of the divine figure.

After having reconstructed the general context, we can now return to grace, because this question can be inferred directly from everything I've just said. What, in short, is the problem posed by grace? The problem is that a divine intervention is needed in order for a creature, a man, to have faith and be saved. Salvation does not lie in the dependence, the benevolence of man alone; it requires a divine intervention, and this divine intervention is the grace that God grants us, which gives us—or, for that matter, does *not* give us—the possibility of faith and of salvation.

The problem of grace is part of the general context that I just reconstructed, because men are in the position of objects vis-à-vis God's plans, will, or desire (Malebranche uses all three terms). The question is obviously how men, being objects of God's desire, can respond to this desire, that is, can subjectivize this position. Let's review the nature of the problem. God declared his plan. He declared it, in particular, in planning for men to become sinners and fallen men, hence in reducing them to nothing and plunging them into the abyss. That is the declaration of his desire. And the status of man, a sinner wandering the earth, is truly the manifestation of this declaration. God could have prevented all of this, but he did not do so because he declared his desire. And so the human condition is itself produced by this declaration. We might even say that it *is* this very declaration. Men are therefore the objects of God's desire in a radical sense: their condition and situation are merely figurations of the divine desire. They themselves have no chance of being a cause of their soul's movement toward God. For their condition in the strictest sense of the term—to be sinners, humiliated, fallen—is to be the effect of a divine declaration. The problem can therefore be formulated like so: How can man (humanity, each man) desire to be the proper object of God's desire, that is, desire to be part of his Church (which is the same thing)? In effect, to desire to be the proper object of God's desire is to desire to be part of his Church since, ultimately, the Church, with Christ as its head, is really the object of God's desire. It is therefore to desire to contribute to the glory of God.

The problem is not so much that men contribute to his glory; it's that they *desire* to contribute to it. This is precisely what distinguishes someone who is saved from someone who isn't. Now, in order to desire to be the adequate object of God's desire, Malebranche says there only two procedures, which, as we'll see, have an impact on the typology of grace: we need either enlightenment—clear thinking— or a feeling, a delectation. Whence the subtle distinctions and the extraordinary subjective difference between the grace of enlightenment and the grace of delectation. We need enlightenment in order to gain insight into the fact that God is our good, that is, to teach us that we have to desire to be the proper object of God's desire. Or else, says Malebranche, we need a feeling that convinces us of it. But ultimately only God can cause this enlightenment or this feeling.

Here, however, we encounter a small complication. By causing this enlightenment or this feeling in men, God in a certain sense revises his declaration, provided we admit that his declaration, the declaration of his plan, was to plunge us into the abyss. This will require a sophisticated dialectic that I'll come back to. But what we must keep in mind for the time being is that grace—what's called grace—is that production of an enlightenment or a feeling through which we desire to be the object of God's desire, which we could not produce on our own. It's very clear here that God is playing with mankind. This is the playful structure of his desire. In short, grace is the production by God (who alone can act in this regard) of an enlightenment or a feeling in our souls, through which we desire to be the proper object of God's desire. This can be put another way: grace is how God calls on us to desire with all our heart to be the objects that cause his own desire to desire. It is how God calls on us to desire to be those objects that act as the cause of his desire to desire.

In a more ontological form, we can say that we're coming back here to the paradox of the object, as it operates throughout this analysis—the paradox of the finite object, of the *objet a*, hence, in this case, of the human soul, which suspends it between being and not-being. Indeed, on the one hand, the object must be—there must be some being of the object—and this is why the world was really created, as God confided to us. There must be a being of the object, because there must be an other. However, we can also say there is a not-being of the object, since this other is the other of being, the other of God. Therefore, in a way, this being is actually a being of not-being. At this point—that is, after a first spiral of this paradox that always places the object in eclipse, in suspense between being and not-being—we can also say this: not to be, for a human soul, is not to be the object of God's desire. This is another formulation of its not-being, since what creates its being is precisely to be the object of God's desire. So if the soul is not the object of God's desire, it is led back to not-being. And Malebranche says clearly that, after the Fall but before Christ, in that temporal interval, which is more-over insignificant for God but not for men, what happens is that men are not objects of God's desire.

After the Fall God, as God, has no relationship with us: mankind is utterly abandoned.

It might be objected that there are prophets nonetheless. But prophets are something else. Prophets are those who announce that God *might* have a relationship with us again someday. But for Malebranche, unlike Pascal, this is not an ambiguous message. The prophets represent a sort of document on this obscure time, at best a series of announcements on the fact that there was indeed a declaration of God's plan. Every time Malebranche speaks about the Old Testament, it is to show and to verify that the Fall and what followed was really the declaration of God's desire. Basically, God cut off his relationship with us after the Fall. He reduced us to the mere status of those through whom his desire is declared. But during that period of time, men are not obliged to be the objects of his desire; they are only the declaration of his desire. Malebranche puts it this way: "In addition it was necessary that after the advent of sin, God have no further consideration of our wills."[2] During said period, he can suddenly become irritable and partially exterminate us; he is no longer interested in us at all. As a human singularity not in God's general plan, we fell outside of his representation and his interest, because we did not have the desire to be in the position of object. That's why, strictly speaking, during this period (and even beyond it for those who are not saved), "not to be" is truly "not to be the object of God's desire." On the other hand, we could say that "to be," for the human soul, is to be the object of God's desire. Grace is ultimately the way God makes the being of his desire dependent on the not-being of our existence. It will mediate the paradox of the object, because it will give rise in us to the human desire to be an object of God's desire, and because in this way we will at least have this being, which is to be connected to the being of God's desire. This is why I would say that grace is what gives us a "quasi-being."

Later I will explain why the problem of grace was so crucial in the seventeenth century. We will deal with the heart of the question, what is most radical about it, when we come to the doctrine of the human subject, which is a question that underlies this edifice. For the time being we are still dealing with the broadest ontological categories. The heart of the debate about grace in the seventeenth century is that, precisely then, a host of terms relevant to the modern doctrine of the subject would be established. This concerned questions of consciousness, freedom, and so on, but above all, the question of what a Christian subject is under conditions in which it can no longer be defined by a stable, hierarchical order, under conditions in which it has become a substantial figure. It, too, would have to be defined as a subject, and the question of grace was decisive for thinking the constitution of this subject.

Grace, we said, is what gives us a quasi-being, i.e., at least the desire to be the object of God's desire. It is how not-being comes to the being of the Church, because the Church is the world insofar as it is the scene of God's glory, insofar as it *is*. All the rest, if I can put it this way, is the world insofar as it is not. And when we are touched by grace, we have that quasi-being that pulls us out of not-being by connecting us to the maximum of being that the not-being of the world is capable of, namely the Church, the temple of God's glory. Finally, the problem of grace is what I'd call the problem of the subject-object, eclipsed in the other's desire. This, for example, might lead us to think that, for Malebranche, every man is a woman for God. We will see in what sense. The problem of the subject-object is that of a subject, whose purpose is to be called on to desire to be the object of the other's desire. And the fact is, to be touched by grace is nothing other than to desire to be the object of God's desire. It is therefore a subject whose figure of actualization is the object, a subject that must come to be in the position of an object.

There are still two major problems that Malebranche will tackle. The first is: Does grace obey laws? God dispenses grace, but *how* does he dispense it? This question was at the time the focus of very heated debates. Is the dispensation of grace part of the unfathomable mystery of God's plans, or are there discernible laws, intelligible to us, of this dispensation? This is the age-old problem: Why was so-and-so, a good, decent man, not saved, while some scoundrel, ultimately converted by an amazing grace, was? Since no one ventured the hypothesis of a truly evil God, the explanation was either because we cannot fathom the ultimate reason for God's plan, or because perhaps no one is saved. Or—and this is the Jesuit thesis—because everyone is saved. This is the famous thesis of an empty hell, which has recently been revived. . . . As you know, modern Christianity doesn't much care for the notion of hell. So theologians have come up with the rather fascinating doctrine that contends that there is indeed an infernal place, but that there's no one in it. Malebranche's thesis will be that there are laws. By virtue of the aesthetic character of ontology, the dispensation of grace will obey general rules. This doesn't mean, however, that we know what these laws are, as is the case with a number of the general laws of nature. Always respectful of authority, Malebranche won't say that we know what all the laws of grace are. That would be to put ourselves a little too quickly in God's place. But he will maintain absolutely that there are general laws of the dispensation of grace, and that these laws, just like the laws of nature, obey the principle of the simplicity of ways. Such is the maximal hypothesis that can and should be put forward.

The second problem is that these general rules are dictated by occasions. The fact that there is a general rule does not prevent us from considering the particular cases in which it acts as a rule, because the laws of grace are, truly, the effective dispensation of grace. You can't know that there is a general rule if you don't observe the particular occasions on which this rule appears as a rule. Let's focus once more on an example from nature: the collision of bodies. A billiard ball hits another billiard ball, and the other ball moves. For Malebranche, there is no question of the billiard ball having the power to move the other billiard ball. Only God acts. Therefore, the action, the observable movement, is really caused by God. And since the law is a general and regular one, on every occasion of this sort, the law comes into play. As a result, a billiard ball will never hit another ball without this second ball moving. That would obviously be to disrupt the general order of God's volitions. For Malebranche, the collision itself is an occasional cause. Not a true cause, not an active cause, since it is not, strictly speaking, the collision that makes the other ball move; it is God. Quite fortunately for us, God always makes the second ball move when there is a collision. So we can still do physics! Of course, if this depended every time on a particular will of God, we most certainly could *not* do physics, since sometimes the ball would move, and sometimes it would not. If there can be physics, it is because we know that with every occasional cause, and therefore with every representable figuration, the law is general. It is therefore possible to reason as if it was really the first ball that made the other one move. But the line is very fine. Since the billiard ball, as a pure portion of extension, has no energy in itself that would allow it to make other balls move, it is not true that it acts: it is God who acts.

But, all things considered, if you reason as if it were truly the ball that acts, it amounts to the same thing, because God won't deviate from his own general will. He won't bother to intervene in such a trifling matter: he determined, once and for all, that this or that will happen, and from then on he is no longer concerned with it, so to speak. In reality, he does actively concern himself each time there is a collision, but he concerns himself with it in the same way every time. Therefore, we can do physics.

The problem is whether we can do the physics of grace! In short, are there occasional causes of grace that would allow us to say that in such and such a case God bestows grace? It is clear that the notions of general will and occasional cause are closely linked, because to say there is a general will is to say that there is a rule, and that on every occasion corresponding to the rule, the rule is at work. But how can we know that the occasions of grace are those occasions on which God makes the rules and laws of its dispensation come into play? We have no trouble understanding that there must be figurable or representable causes of divine action as regulated action. We know what natural causes are, and it is in that context that the laws of physics are established. We can easily identify all the occasional causes regarding which divine action regularly comes into play. With grace, it's the same problem: What are the occasions regarding which God dispenses grace, and according to what general principle does he do so? To get a clear picture of grace we must be able to identify those occasions regarding which God dispenses his grace, and to know what general principle this dispensation obeys.

Let's begin with the general rules. Malebranche's motivation is the same here as it is for nature: it would be inaesthetic for grace to be arbitrary. And it would be unworthy of God to act in a given circumstance through a particular will. God himself (we'll see how this "God himself" complicates things considerably; we'll need to strictly distinguish God from Christ) is not particularly interested in the salvation of this or that person. The general structure of his desire for glory does not directly involve the question of whether Denise or Paul is going to hell or somewhere else. As Malebranche says quite emphatically, all of these things are only the materials needed for his glory. So there's no reason to think that there are particular wills of God in a given circumstance. There are therefore general rules. We should assume them a priori, and what should be thought is the connection between grace and glory, for that is where general laws are determined. This is explicitly expressed in the metaphor of the temple and its ornaments, a key example in Malebranche's aesthetic ontology. Let me read you a passage:

> That which makes the beauty of a temple is in the order and the variety of the ornaments which come together in it. Thus, to render the living temple of the majesty of God worthy of him who must inhabit it, and proportioned to the wisdom and to the infinite love of its author, there are no beauties that ought not to be found there. But it is not the same with this temple raised to the glory of God as with material temples. That which constitutes the beauty of the spiritual edifice of the Church is the infinite diversity of the graces which he who is the head of it distributes to all the parts that compose it: it is the order and the admirable relations which he places

between them: these are the different degrees of glory which shine from all sides.[3]

It is clear that, in the context of Malebranche's aesthetic, the distribution of graces, their infinite variety, should not be related to the salvation of this or that person, but to the degree of glory that results from this distribution.

The second point is that there should be a legal agreement between the order of grace and the order of nature. There, too, the motivation is strictly aesthetic, but we have seen the extent to which the aesthetic is a doctrine of being for Malebranche. The principle of the simplicity of ways should be extended to the relationship between nature and grace; it would not be harmonious for nature and grace to obey two entirely heterogeneous principles. If they can obey the same principles, it would naturally be more glorious, since it is important to minimize being vis-à-vis the ornamentation of nothingness. As a result, God must be thrifty in the dispensation of grace; he must produce a maximum of effects of grace with a minimum of decisions and principles. This is what will make it possible to harmonize the order of grace and the order of nature. Here is how Malebranche formulates it:

> Since it is the same God who is the author of the order of grace and of that of nature, it is necessary that these two orders be in agreement with respect to everything they contain, which marks the wisdom and the power of their author. Thus, since God is a general cause whose wisdom has no limits, it is necessary for the reasons which I stated before, that in the order of grace as well as in that of nature, he acts as a general cause; and that having as his end his glory in the construction of his Church, he establish the simplest and the most general laws, which have by their effect the greatest amount of wisdom and of fruitfulness.[4]

So we see that on the question of grace there are exactly the same principles and axioms as on the question of nature and that the order of grace must be homogeneous with the order of nature in aesthetic terms.

The consequences will nevertheless be more troublesome in the order of grace than in the order of nature, and Malebranche will have to deal with two important problems.

The first problem: The Church has always maintained that God wanted all men to be saved. There are any number of texts on God's goodness, and ultimately, the essence of God's goodness is that God sincerely wants all men to be saved. However, it's clear that not everyone has faith; therefore, God has not given sufficient grace to everyone. How can this be reconciled with his supreme goodness? This is the problem of the general laws of grace. We could easily imagine a very simple general law, which would be that everyone receives sufficient grace. Obviously, it is not this law that's at work here. Malebranche's answer is that the dispensation of grace can only be general provided that there are men who do not benefit from it. The generality of the dispensation of grace, which takes precedence over everything because it is the aesthetics of being, can produce maximally varied effects (which is the law of the world) only provided that not everyone is saved. God could of course give sufficient grace to everyone, but he could only do so by adding a particular decision to his general decisions, by supplementing the general legislation with a particular decision. But his wisdom won't allow him to do so. Don't forget that wisdom is the structure of his desire. Malebranche has a striking phrase about God: "His Wisdom renders him, so to speak, powerless."[5] This has significant implications. This apparent weakness of God refers to the structured nature of his desire, which means that there can be fullness or completion of the object—and therefore general salvation—only through an inflation of particular wills.

Here's another objection along the same lines: the question of the Fall and of sin again. To the extent that God was able to plan the Fall and sin, the fact that there was a risk of having lost souls was foreseeable, and that's an imperfection. To which Malebranche's response, which I've already discussed at some length: "God loves his Wisdom even more than his work."[6] This should be understood to mean: he prefers his own desire to the object of his desire. This would lead us—and I might come back to it—to the question of love in Malebranche. Love and desire are not the same thing, and they're not the same thing for Malebranche either. Which, incidentally, doesn't mean that God desires his wisdom even more than his work, which wouldn't mean much, for in reality the cause of his desire—what he desires—is indeed his work, namely, Christ on the cross, hence himself on the cross. But what Malebranche says is that God loves his wisdom even more than his desire, his wisdom even more than his image.

At this juncture, after the metaphor of the temple, we come to the metaphor of the rain. I said that the second great metaphor of the *Treatise on Nature and Grace* is the rain. Grace will fall like the rain, that is to say, in a general way, which has nothing to do with what it falls on. Malebranche comes back to this constantly in the *Treatise on Nature and Grace*: it rains just as much on the sea as it does on the desert sands, whereas there are fertile lands on which not a drop of rain falls. Likewise, grace falls on hardened and stubborn hearts who make no use of it, and not on tender hearts who would really need it and would make good use of it. It falls like the rain, according to its own law, which is not the law of its destination. Its own law is the intrinsic beauty of this law itself.

Malebranche writes: "In matters of grace, God undoes and redoes without cease."[7] Obviously—since there are always souls that should be saved who aren't, grace having fallen awry, etc. To all appearances, the work of salvation is thus a sort of endless Penelopean work, where God weaves and unweaves, braids and rebraids without end. Now this is due to the fact that there is no particular action in this, but only what Malebranche calls the laws of grace. Let me read you a passage:

> Thus as one has no right to be annoyed that the rain falls in the sea where it is useless, and that it does not fall on seeded grounds where it is necessary—because the laws of the communication of motion are simple, quite fruitful, and perfectly worthy of the wisdom of their author, and because according to these laws it is not possible that rain be distributed on the earth rather than in the seas—so too one ought not to complain of the apparent irregularity according to which grace is given to men. It is the regularity with which God acts, it is the simplicity of the laws which he observes, it is the wisdom and the uniformity of his conduct, which is the cause of that apparent irregularity. It is necessary, according to the laws of grace, that God has ordained, on behalf of his elect and for the building of his Church, that this heavenly rain sometimes fall on hardened hearts, as well as on prepared grounds. If, then, grace falls uselessly, it is not the case that God acts without design. It is still less the case that God acts with the aim of making men more guilty through the abuse of his favors. Rather the simplicity of general laws does not permit that this grace, which is inefficacious in this corrupted heart, fall in another heart where it would be efficacious. This grace not being given at all by a particular will, but in consequence of the immutability of the general order of grace, it suffices that that order produce a work proportioned to the simplicity of his laws, in order that it be worthy of the wisdom of its author. For finally the order of grace would be less perfect, less admirable, less lovable, if it were more complex.[8]

Two considerations can be drawn from the use of this metaphor.

First, an aesthetic consideration, which I have amply stressed: it is the general order that has precedence, because this is where the beauty of the thing comes from. Then there is a consideration that is very typical of God's relationship to men in Malebranche's thought: since men are objects of God's desire, it is important that they understand that it is the general structure of God's desire that is at stake and that they ought not ask for particular favor. They ought not ask that they be given grace because they might need it, because God's desire is a general one, and to ask for particular favor is to fail to recognize God's desire, to disregard God's desire.

The object of God's desire is the general nothingness of humanity, which is the scene of his victim fantasy, the nothingness in which he will represent himself on the cross. This is how he attains his structured desire, that is, his wisdom and glory, which we can now say is the name of his *jouissance*. If we wanted to transpose Malebranche's terminology, in a slightly mechanical way perhaps, we would ultimately have to say this: wisdom is really God's desire, and glory is his *jouissance*. Now, in view of all this, a man's specific request simply makes no sense. The object that man is can be called or elected, he will or he will not receive grace; he can be elected in a given circumstance, but always in conformity with a law, a rule, never on the basis of his singularity.

The first problem thus concerns the general aesthetic of grace and the futility of every particular request. The second problem will concern the question of what provides an occasion for the generality of the law of grace, of what ensures that there is an effectivity of grace, what ensures that grace is actually dispensed. I explained to you a little while ago that there must be regular occasions in order for us to observe that a law is a law, something that, in nature, being of the order of the representable, doesn't pose too many problems. But in the order of grace what provides an occasion for the laws of grace to manifest themselves as laws? This is much more complicated, because it is definitely not of the order of the sensible, of the order of the directly representable.

What can the occasional cause of grace possibly be? I will only touch on the problem, but we'll see that it will lead us into the heart of a very fascinating investigation. The obvious solution would be to say that the occasional cause of grace is quite simply men's behavior. This does not amount to saying that someone who's good will automatically receive grace, while someone who's bad won't. We don't have a clue about that; these are the general laws of grace. But that doesn't mean we can't imagine that what gives grace the occasion to manifest itself is the way men act, think, relate to the Church, and so on. The occasional cause might be, for example, the sinner's temptation. Being exposed to temptation—what a wonderful occasional cause! That is, every time I'm exposed to temptation, grace descends, just as every time a ball is hit by another one, it moves. For Malebranche, this is the same type of problem. It might also be the desire for grace, that is, the will, or the desire, to be the object of God's desire, that would provide the occasion for grace to comfort, strengthen, and support him. This doctrine seems at first glance obvious and simple: just as certain material configurations are occasions for the laws of nature, so, too, certain spiritual configurations might be occasions for the laws of grace. We would thus have the impression of a well-ordered temple. But Malebranche absolutely refuses this hypothesis. This is not at all the path he will go down, and he will even—through the mechanism of compounding problems, as is his wont—explicitly refute this point. The occasional cause of grace can in no case be ourselves. Here is what he writes:

> However, since grace is not given to all those who wish for it, nor as soon as they wish for it, and since it is given to those who do not ask for it, it follows that even our desires are not at all the occasional

causes of grace. For these sorts of causes always have their effect very promptly, and without them the effect is never produced. For example, the collision of bodies being the occasional cause of the change which takes place in their motion, if two bodies do not meet, their motion changes not at all, and if they change, one can be assured that the bodies have met. The general laws which diffuse grace in our hearts, thus find nothing in our wills which determine their efficacy—just as the general laws which govern the rains are not based on the dispositions of the places where it rains. For whether the grounds be fallow or whether they be cultivated, it rains indifferently in all places, both in the deserts and in the sea.[9]

So Malebranche explicitly rules out the thesis that would make subjective disposition the occasional cause of grace. If such were the case, grace would manifest itself without fail. It would need to work like the collision of bodies. Now, it is neither because we desire grace that we have it, nor because we are worthy, nor because we are sinners. What we see, with regard to our subjective disposition, is a capricious appearance, an appearance of complete autonomy, as with the rain. The souls that grace falls upon are not occasional causes of grace, because there is no regular relation, and because "occasional cause" means an infallible relation or, as Malebranche says, an "immediate relation." God does not waste time: he acts as soon as there is the figure of the occasional cause.

If the spiritual figures of the human subject are not the occasional causes of grace, things become very complicated. What can the occasional cause of grace possibly be? Because, —I must stress this—there must be one. If there isn't one, it is impossible to understand in what sense it's an effective general will, a real law, which manifests itself without fail before a given phenomenon. Apparently, neither the state of bodies nor the state of souls elicits the regulated intervention of God. The solution Malebranche will propose is to say that the occasional cause of grace is the soul of Christ. So it is indeed in connection with the soul that things happen, but here it's a very specific soul, the soul of Christ—the soul, it could be said, of a third party between men and God, of someone eccentric in relation to both man and God, while at the same taking part in both. For Christ is God as finite, as man. Let me remind you in passing of that completely remarkable doctrine, which is that grace is God's intervening so that we might desire to be the object of his desire. And what Malebranche says is that the subject-object, that is, the person who desired to be the other's object of desire, is consistent with this desire of the other—with God's desire—only insofar as a third party proposes this consistency. And it is Christ who will propose—to propose is to be the occasion for—the dispensation of grace to a particular individual. And he does so simply because he thinks about him or her. Every time Christ thinks about someone, grace falls, without fail, upon him or her; i.e., the general law of grace will manifest itself. So the apparent irregularity is in fact a regularity, because Christ, being the universal mediator, thinks about everyone, about a hardened heart and a prepared soul alike.

But then why does grace not come to everyone, since he thinks about everyone? The answer is absolutely extraordinary here: Christ as man, and therefore as finite soul, although eternal, cannot think about everyone at the same time. He thinks in principle about everyone, and perhaps over the centuries he will end up having thought about many people, because, as a finite but eternal soul, he is coextensive with the world. Whence the purely apparent capriciousness of grace, whose final foundation is simply the benevolence of Christ, a universal but finite benevolence. Christ is apprehended here from the perspective of his being as the occasional cause of grace, that is, in his explicit function as mediator. He is in fact the mediator or the third party who, just by the thought he has about a particular situation, causes God to dispense upon this particular situation the grace of being the object of his desire. It is therefore in the strict sense that we can say that he is a third party who proposes a man's conformity to God's desire, a conformity that seals, validates, and indicates the descent of grace.

All this will pose considerable problems, the core of which is Christ's third-party position in the structure of God's desire. This is different from what we've already seen, namely, Christ as object of God's desire. It is not directly and explicitly the same thing, even though, as we'll see, it still contributes to glory; the thread is never lost. But here Christ has another role: he is the occasional cause of grace. This is not the same as being in the role of purpose and general object of God's desire, as God crucified.

So, can I do something to make Christ think about me? To attract his attention? This means, in a certain sense: can I seduce Christ? This will be mediated by another factor, which is the possible existence of a specific desire of Christ himself. That's why I said that it was really another role. Up to now, Christ was the figuration of the object of God's desire, whereas if we enter into the question of Christ's own desire, we will find that this desire is to save all men. But what is the role of his desire to save all men—a desire that acts, in this case, by particular thoughts? Christ's "all men" is not the same as God's "all men." God certainly wants to save all men, but this is part of the aesthetics of his plan, whereas Christ truly wants to save them all. Only he doesn't have enough time. This question, presented the way I'm presenting it here, might sound funny, but we will see that, as usual with Malebranche, the categories at work are at the same time very interesting and anticipate a number of considerations. Indeed, the introduction of the parameter of time—the time of the soul, the time of the subject— will lead to some very significant paradoxes, which in turn will lead the infinite-finite relationship to interact with the eternity-time relationship. For if the infinite-finite relationship in some sense controls the dialectic of nature, the eternity-time relationship controls the dialectic of grace.

I would like to conclude this discussion by pointing out that we are touching here on the polyvalence of Christ. Christ is a multi-functional term. And we are going to take up the consideration of a second function of Christ, his mediating role, where he is the occasional cause: his role as head of the Church. Up to now, Christ was the architect of the eternal Temple. Now we'll switch from his role as architect of the eternal Temple, which refers to the general structure of God's desire, to his role as head of the Church, which is responsible for the particular salvation of men. As head of the Church, Christ must care for his entire flock. This is really a different role, a different dialectic, which we'll examine next time.

Session 6

May 6, 1986

We had begun to examine what the occasional cause of the dispensation of grace is. Let me remind you of the broad outlines of the problem. It is clear that grace is dispensed according to its own laws, which obey the aesthetic principles of the general will and the simplicity of ways. There is consequently no question of God dispensing grace on a case-by-case basis, according to the particular situation of the person to whom grace is given. Grace is like the rain: it is not dispensed on the basis of whatever it falls upon; it is dispensed in accordance with its own system of legality.

As a result, it is completely pointless to hope to know why grace is dispensed in particular cases. Which, moreover, has nothing to do with a mystery but rather with the fact that the knowledge in question is a knowledge of laws, not of details. What we can know at the very least is that the dispensation is regulated, that it is subject to a law. This maxim should therefore be considered not as a maxim of ignorance but as a maxim of mathematization. Just as mathematics, as Malebranche thinks it, is not the knowledge of specific things but of general essences, so, too, the knowledge we have of grace is not a knowledge of the details of particular dispensations but the knowledge of laws. It is very important to understand that Malebranche's project is a mathematization of the principles of the question of grace and not at all a position concerning the unfathomable mystery of God. In other words, he is explicitly concerned with extending the Galilean movement of the mathematization of nature to grace: regularity of things, general simplicity of laws, uniformity of action, etc. That's his way of being modern. This approach is part of the general framework I already mentioned, namely, the attempt to mathematize Christianity itself, thus to incorporate it into modernity. What is completely remarkable is that the mathematization of Christianity in fact means the mathematization of the subject, the matheme of the subject. Since the mathematization of nature is the mathematization of matter, the mathematization of Christianity is necessarily a mathematization of the soul, of salvation, and finally of God, his calculations, and his project. The aim is truly a sort of matheme of the subject, which is why we constantly find correspondences in Malebranche with the most complex and compelling contemporary theories of the subject, especially Lacan's.

The mathematization of grace, which is at the heart of the question of the existence of a matheme of the subject, will find its point of maximum complexity in the question of the occasional cause. It can be formulated like this: on what occasion is grace dispensed according to its own law? What induces the law to be efficacious? It is not enough to say that the law is general. We must know how we gain access to this generality, and therefore what the circumstance—the occasion—is that, consistently and without exception this time, induces the dispensation of grace. So long as you have not understood this issue, to say that grace is dispensed according to general laws is to some extent meaningless. The same is true of grace as of nature: the generality of the law must be confirmed one way or another in experience. There must be an experience of the regularity of the law so that we can maintain that the law is effectively regular. Otherwise, the hypothesis is meaningless.

You will not have solved the problem of the mathematization of grace if you have not solved the problem of its occasion, that is, of the circumstances in which this grace is actually distributed according to its law. You can certainly say that God is the consistent cause of movement, but physics is only possible because he is the consistent cause of movement in accordance with certain occasions. If one billiard ball hits another, there is necessarily movement: to an occasion x an effect y must correspond.

But on what occasion is grace dispensed? This is the key issue of the *Treatise on Nature and Grace*, and it is simultaneously the trickiest and riskiest issue. Indeed, we come up against the intricacies of the matheme of the subject, because grace is a subjective phenomenon. Malebranche's demonstration will start from a lemma, a general statement that enhances the aesthetic—an aesthetic and therefore ontological lemma, since aesthetics and ontology are finally the same thing for him—in order to end up, as I said last time, with the fundamental thesis that the occasional cause of grace is Christ.

Let's begin with the lemma that will govern the demonstration. An occasional cause, Malebranche maintains, cannot be entirely separated from the field of the effects of the cause, of the real cause, namely, divine action or intervention. In other words, it is impossible for there not to be any thinkable relationship between the occasional cause and the lawful action of God. This postulation has two sides to it. An aesthetic side, first of all, as is usual with Malebranche. In fact, an occasional cause that had nothing to do with the divine intervention's field of effects (i.e., if the occasion on which God acted had nothing to do with why he acted) would clearly have something inharmonious, even arbitrary, about it. For example, Malebranche will say (targeting, among other things, all the kinds of supposed cosmic clairvoyance and horoscopes): "God has not taken . . . the course of the planets as occasional causes of the union of our soul with our body."[1] If the charlatans of fortune-telling were right, it would mean that when Mars enters the constellation of Leo, such or such phenomenon occurs at the junction of my body and my soul. That's astrology. That astrology comes immediately to Malebranche's mind as an inaesthetic, and therefore illegitimate, example is really remarkable.

This leads to the second feature of this lemma: it is an anti-obscurantist lemma. Indeed, the radical disjunction between the occasional cause and the field of effects is one possible definition of obscurantism; that would at any rate be its Malebranchian definition. If you think that the configuration of the stars determines loves, that would certainly be inaesthetic in Malebranche's eyes but above all completely obscurantist, since there is no thinkable connection between the two phenomena. Here's another example, but it's striking to see that it is in fact the same one: "Thus the rain of Grace," he writes, "is not diffused in our hearts according to the different situations of the stars. . . ."[2] Once again, astrology is called into question, or raised to the status of a paradigm of what cannot partake in divine action. Astrology existed and had already had a long history behind it, and so the stakes were polemical. It is the figure of Malebranche's rationalism—an aesthetic rationalism, but rationalism all the same—that is at stake in this matter. There must be a representable connection between the occasional cause and the effects that are spoken of. If it's the union of the soul and the body you're talking about, this should entail the sphere of feelings, emotions, etc., not of the conjunction of the stars. Likewise for the rain of grace, which concerns subjects and not the movement of the moon and cosmography.

Underlying this, we find, as against the globalizing short-circuits, a theory of the local nature, of the local connectedness of things, including of divine action. We could even say in summary that divine action is always relational. It has a topology; it has local requisites. Malebranche explicitly develops the point of view according to which, when you claim to explain something by connecting it to the divine will, you have thought nothing at all, and when you say about such or such a phenomenon (including an apparently miraculous one) "It's like that because God willed it, it is the will of God," this is an empty thought. You have thought nothing because this is obvious. And the same holds for everything. Since God alone acts, it is possible to say that any phenomenon whatsoever occurs because God willed it. To say such a thing amounts to saying "Being is being, being is what it is, God is God." It's an empty tautology. Thinking begins only when I think the local connection. Thinking the immediate, transitive relationship of the global structure to the local is not thinking. Since everything is God's desire, everything is situated in the space of the global structure. Thinking demands that we determine a localization of what we think. This topological vision of knowledge is very interesting. For Malebranche, knowledge is not the subsumption of the local by the global, which is a universally valid maxim and therefore completely uninteresting. Every problem is particular; every problem involves some discovery, some determination of a local connection. If, for example, I am looking for the occasional cause of grace, I must solve the particular problem it poses. In saying that the cause of grace is God I have said nothing at all. This is a very strong feeling in Malebranche's work and, in a certain sense, it is also from this that he draws his scientific inspiration, his general project of mathematization. There are real problems, but insofar as you have not formulated them, you haven't thought anything at all yet; you have only repeated the global structure. And repeating the global structure is tautological.

If we now return to the problem of grace armed with the conviction that there must be a connection, and that we will never find the original cause of grace in the movements of the stars, the configuration of the planet, or the growth of plants, etc., grace will have to be found in something that has a connection with the problem. Now, grace is men's relationship to the Church. As I explained last time, grace is divine intervention applied to a very specific issue: men's desire to be objects of God's desire. Grace is what God dispenses to help men to be such that their desire is to be objects of God's desire. So we can say that, in reality, grace concerns intersubjectivity, that is, the question of the alignment of two desires. A state of grace is the alignment of two desires—in this case, a god's desire and a man's desire. Should we go so far as to say that every state of grace includes something that resembles a god? That remains to be seen!

For Malebranche, at any rate, grace is an attribute of intersubjectivity, something that has to do with the communication of desires and therefore, ultimately, with the complex dialectic of desire as the key site of the Other's desire. The result is that if we try to find what the occasional cause of grace is, it necessarily concerns one of the two terms "the Church" or "men," since grace is the reason why a man is helped by being in the Church. Now we know that the Church is, among things of the world, the object of God's desire. The Church is Christ or, more precisely, the world becoming Christ, and the world exists only because there was the project of the Church. Since God created the world in order for there to be his Church, the latter becomes the meaning of the world, hence God in the world, God made man. Ultimately, the Church is Christ, in the dimension of his body, in the dimension of his worldly finitude. We might say—and it has often been said—in a nutshell that the Church is the body of God. But let me remind you that the "body of God" implies all the truths I've spoken about: the becoming-nothing of being, namely, the body and finitude. Here again is the traditional designation of the Church as the mystical body of Christ. And so grace is the reason why a man is part of this body, participates in this mystical body of Christ—why he is, as Malebranche will say, one of the materials of this body. We also know that he often thinks this body as a metaphor of the temple. The local connection we need to solve the problem of the occasional cause of grace should be sought, since it does not lie solely in the action of men, in Christ, insofar as the Church is his body.

Incidentally, the effectuation of grace, the effect of grace, is really to be part of the body of Christ. So it is an incorporation. God's desire clearly has something cannibalistic about it. The ritual, the Catholic ritual, is symbolically cannibalistic: God's body is ingested through the host. But this ingestion of God's body should be understood the other way around: in the communion, it is a matter of becoming a part of this body oneself, of being ingested oneself by God's body. The central question of the Eucharist is in reality: who ingests whom? Ultimately, it is Christ who ingests men, even though the physical appearance of the Eucharist suggests that it is men who ingest Christ. "This is my body" means: my body is intended for you. It's clear that the remainder of our question— what is the occasional cause of grace?—is played out between men, who must desire to be incorporated into the Church, and Christ, who is the body of this Church.

From there, Malebranche proceeds primarily by elimination, refuting the idea that the occasional cause can be men. I refer you to the passage where this refutation occurs, namely, Paragraph 6 of the Second Discourse, a passage I read to you during our last session, and from which I'm extracting the following sentence, so that you really have it in your memory: "The general laws which diffuse grace in our hearts, thus find nothing in our wills which determine their efficacy."[3] Our wills, our desires—these words are actually used— do not induce the dispensation of grace. They are not its occasional cause because, let's not forget, the occasional cause is necessarily infallible; and because, if there is an occasion, there must be an effect. Otherwise, it would be impossible to speak of a general law. Given that when we desire grace it is absolutely uncertain whether we'll obtain it, our desire must be disqualified as occasional cause.

Malebranche will also show that the temptation we are exposed to is not an occasional cause either, the proof being that we often succumb to it. Nevertheless, this does not prove that there has been no dispensation of grace, or even an insufficient amount of grace; it only proves that it's not where we should look for the occasional cause of grace. At a deep level, this means that in order for a subject to be the other's object of desire, it is not enough for the subject to desire it. This is quite true and testifies to a great subtlety in the substructure of the theology on the question of the subject. There is no doubt that, in order to be adequate to the other's desire, it is not enough to desire it, and it is on this observation that Malebranche will base his disqualification of the subject, the human subject, as inducing grace.

Insofar as neither the temptation to which we are exposed nor the desire or will to be saved, to receive grace, thus to enter living into God's desire—none of that—can function as the occasional cause of the dispensation of grace in terms of a general law, the cause must necessarily be Christ. Incidentally, Malebranche gave no positive proof of this point. He proved it through the following process: since there must be a connection, it must either be Christ or men; but since it cannot be men, it is therefore Christ. The reasoning proceeds by elimination, not by affirmative demonstration. Only, as is always the case when you prove something by elimination, Malebranche tries to consolidate his position by its effects, hence to prove that it works. If the occasional cause is Christ, this also means that the fact that the subject can be the adequate object of the other's desire requires the mediation of a third party. In other words, a subject becomes the object of the other's desire only to the extent that it has been indicated by a third party. This is really what's called intercession. Malebranche defends the thesis—which is regarded as a modern one—that every desire requires an intercessor, that the structure of desire is always triangular. Christ will therefore pray to God for men, which means he will select certain men, one man or another, as possible objects of God's desire. That's what intercession is. As a result, grace—namely, the attention of God's desire—will fall on a particular subject, because he or she has been selected by Christ. We will see later on that the principle of selection is a very complicated problem.

For the moment, we are dealing with the general structure. It is important to see, by the way, that Malebranche brings into the thesis (which is, moreover, a general thesis on desire) the role of the third party. In so doing, he exhausted in one fell swoop what someone like René Girard devoted long works to. The third party's role in desire, the idea that what a subject desires of another subject presupposes the desire of a third (which is actually Girard's central thesis) is present in a very crucial way in Malebranche. What is Christ, as mediator? "Mediator": he's always been called that. Malebranche didn't invent it; the Church Fathers had long spoken of him in these terms. The Christ in question is Christ as a man, of course, because an occasional cause is a natural cause. Obviously—because otherwise it would be God, and we'd fall back into the short circuit of obscurantism again. If we take Christ in the sense of his identity with the Father, to say that he's the occasional cause of grace amounts quite simply to saying that the occasional cause of grace is God himself. And according to the principle I laid out for you a moment ago, we will have thought nothing at all. Therefore, it is Christ as man who is in question, the finitude of the infinite, the becoming-finite of the infinite. That Christ is the occasional cause will inscribe him in a second role, the one Malebranche calls "the zeal that Jesus Christ had for the glory of his Father."[4] You'll note how concise Malebranche's axiom is. We always come back to the initial axiom: glory, that is, the service of the Father's desire. And it is in this role that Christ will select the objects of that desire. Christ is a sort of recruiter of souls, so that the Father can notice them and save them.

In the zeal that he relentlessly expends for the glory of his Father, Christ wants the Church to be as ample and magnificent as possible. Consequently, he wants the maximum number of souls to be incorporated into the Church. This is his role as architect of the eternal Temple. Malebranche gets straight to the point: he compares souls to large squared stones and uses the expression "materials." Christ, as builder of the Temple for the glory of the Father, takes these materials, these big squared stones—the souls— and thinks of them and loves them but as an architect loves the stones with which he builds the sumptuous edifice that is his work. Since he wants the Church to be as ample and magnificent as possible, the more he incorporates living souls into this edifice, the more the glory of God will be magnified. But the problem is that we are dealing with Christ as man and, as Malebranche says, "the soul of Jesus Christ has not at all an infinite capacity."[5] If it did have such a capacity, we would end up again with the figure that identifies Christ purely and simply with the Father, the figure that prevents him from being a possible occasional cause and that, once more, by the obscurantist short circuit, takes us back to the abyss of divine infallibility. The architect of the eternal Temple carries out a temporal enterprise, temporal here meaning finite—finite in each of its configurations. This means, we should note, that the Church is a work in progress. It is a not a completed whole; it is a work which, in a way, will be built stone by stone, beginning with the first one: "Upon this rock I will build my Church." Malebranche summarizes Christ's plan in this way:

> Thus, since the soul of Jesus Christ has not at all an infinite capacity, and he wants to place in the body of the Church an infinity of beauties and ornaments, one has every reason to believe that there is in this holy soul a continual chain of thoughts and desires, with respect to the mystical body which it forms without ceasing.[6]

This plan is to accomplish the glory of the Father, and therefore to build the Church with an infinity of beauties and ornaments, which, as is incidentally very clear, are in some sense the maximum being of nothingness. After all, the world—and the Church itself—are nothing compared with God. Now, Malebranche's aesthetic consists precisely in extracting the most being from nothingness: that is what the glory of God is. But since the soul of Christ is finite, this will unfold as a succession of desires, not as a sudden flash. The Church cannot be built in a flash by Christ. It is temporal; it is a work in progress that, in the soul of Christ, appears as a continuous series of thoughts and desires concerning the mystical body it continuously forms.

It is precisely these desires of Christ that will constitute the system of occasional causes of grace. In other words, every time Christ desires something relating to the Church, the laws of grace come into play. Christ's desires are always fulfilled. We should not lose sight of this point, because it will create significant problems for us later on. The Father refuses him nothing: because he truly loves his son; because Christ is an offspring who is pushed into life; because this son is the occasional cause while he, the Father, acts by general will. Therefore, if Christ has a particular desire, the regular effects of grace follow automatically, since he is the occasional cause of grace. We could imagine that the Father refuses him nothing and gives him everything he asks for because he is generous and bound by no law. But it is exactly the opposite: this absence of refusal in fact has to do with divine legality; it is even the height of the law. Since Christ is the occasional cause of the dispensation of grace, the law must necessarily manifest itself every time, and his desires are in some sense the occasion for the law. If he desires something, inasmuch as he desires it only for the Church, the law comes into play and fulfills his desire, thereby creating an absolute homonymy between desire and law in this particular respect. In the reality of the occasional cause, desire and law are absolutely interchangeable.

The problem we run into in this framework is still the fact that there are many people who are not saved. Christ, the occasional cause of grace, does not function in such a way that everyone is saved. This functioning is actually a dysfunctioning since, even though all of Christ's desires are fulfilled, there are nevertheless some people who fall through the cracks. Not everyone can enter the body of the Church. Underlying this problem is an interesting aesthetic consideration: there is no beautiful construction without excess stone; you have to remove it and carve into the material. A magnificent edifice cannot be built by using everything that is at hand. The stones must be squared; they must be made to fit. There are some souls that fit, and others that don't. The beauty of the Temple cannot be achieved without some things being broken. Now, we know God is not at all to blame for all this since he coincides with his desire; and that, nevertheless, the law is the beauty of the eternal Temple because it is the law of the maximum of being from nothingness, and there is a maximum of being from nothingness only provided that there is the nothingness of nothingness. The nothingness of nothingness are the reprobates, the castoffs of glory. And Malebranche sometimes comes quite close to insinuating that this, after all, is their contribution to glory. Certainly, for someone who contributes to glory in this way it can be quite discouraging to be eternally condemned, but he can ultimately console himself by thinking that he is still contributing to glory. Which is basically quite close to Hegel's reflections on the condemned man, which can be found in the dialectic of crime and punishment, in *Elements of the Philosophy of Right*. There, Hegel does not hesitate to say that, fundamentally, the condemned man desires his condemnation, wills his condemnation, because it in this way that the essence of the State appears. Therefore, when he mounts the scaffold, he is the glorious subjective presence of the advent of the subject of the State.

If we approach things from the standpoint of the object of desire, we can see that this vanishing position—which consists in being suspended between being and nothingness and in shining gloriously while at the same time being nothing—appears in the fact that there must necessarily be some elect and some damned; that some are incorporated alive into the body of the Church while others are effectively in the position of being castoffs, in the strictest sense of the term. That's the underlying answer. But Malebranche will express this in a manner better suited to his purposes.

The key is that since Christ does not have an infinite capacity in his soul, there is only a series of desires, a succession, and no one all-encompassing flash. Christ doesn't think of everyone all at once.

Here is what Malebranche writes:

> The different movements of the soul of Jesus Christ being occasional causes of grace, one should not be surprised if it is sometimes given to great sinners, or to persons who will not make the slightest use of it. For the soul of Jesus, thinking to raise a temple of vast extent and of infinite beauty, can wish that grace be given to the greatest sinners: and if at that moment Jesus Christ actually thinks of misers, for example, then misers will receive grace. Or again Jesus Christ having need, for the construction of his Church, of minds of a certain character (which comes about ordinarily only in those who suffer certain persecutions, whereof the passions of men are the natural principle): in a word Jesus Christ having need of minds of a certain character in order to bring about certain effects in his Church, he can in general apply to them, and by that application diffuse in them the grace that sanctifies them—just as the mind of an architect thinks in general of squared stones, for example, when those sorts of stones are presently necessary to his building.[7]

The architect of the eternal Temple, who works in time, thinks at a given moment that one category or another of aesthetic resources are necessary for his work. He thinks in terms of general categories—that is, of the stones he needs, in the given, historically given, state, for his enterprise. And since, like Malebranche, he is a Baroque artist, he sometimes thinks of things that are quite audacious, asymmetries, strange ornaments . . . So we shouldn't think that he's limited to monotony and is always thinking of the good, decent folks, for that would be an aesthetics so poor that it would betray the principle of God's glory. This is the very deep insight that an object of desire matters because of its singularity, that there is no uniform and general category of the object of desire. It's well known that such objects can be peripheral things, totally absurd fetishes. Indeed, there is a Baroque of the object of desire. It's the same thing here. In the service of the Father's desire, the Son can select absurd objects—absurd, at any rate, for those of us who don't understand the overall vision of this architecture. Whence the example given by Malebranche. At a given moment, Christ might think it would be good to incorporate into the body of the Church a number of misers, lechers, prideful or persecuted men, or even non-Christians. And when he thinks of them because they would have a role to play in the work, he is the occasional cause of grace for them. It might happen, of course, that the people in question make no use of this grace, that is, do not incorporate themselves into the edifice of the Church. But they will still have been summoned by Christ to receive the grace that might have incorporated them.

The essence of Malebranche's position on this is based on an aesthetic condition. But there is another condition as well, which concerns the question of temporality. The relationship between the infinite and the finite, which is the relationship between God and world and God and Christ (that is, of God to himself as at once infinite and finite), is projected onto the relationship between eternity and time, which becomes one of the ways this relationship is actualized. As a result, it is essential that the work of God, as world and therefore as Church, be temporal. Christ is the mediation of time in God's desire. But what Malebranche sees with considerable insight is that this function of time is actually the point where the ideal object is generated. The ideal object is the asymptotic perspective of the completed Church. But naturally the completed Church is also the completion of time itself; it is not only the Church that is asymptotic. Malebranche writes: "the mystical body of Jesus Christ is not yet a perfect man, and will only be such at the end of time."[8] This man who will be "perfect . . . at the end of time" is, at the termination of time, the completed glory of God, his perfect glory, everything he is capable of in terms of glory, and therefore an object totally adequate to his desire. Only, as we know, an object totally adequate to his desire means desire itself. And Malebranche knows this very well because, finally, this completed Church is not an object, it is an ideal, an asymptotic ideal. Christ is really the one who is governed by this ideal, who works ceaselessly toward the unachievable completion of the Church. In terms of aesthetics, the work, as it is conceived of here, is a modern work, because it is a work that cannot be completed, *a work in progress*.

In this context, we can ask what the resurrection of the dead means. It is in reality the time of the "perfect man," at the end of time, and therefore we know nothing about it. It is the ideal object, the moment when, in a certain way, the glory of God will have completed its cycle. Perhaps God will have another idea, because, otherwise, he might be seriously bored. Indeed, if by chance this ideal were to come about, God would be eliminated; there would be no more God as subject. There is indeed an ideal that God should no longer be a subject, because the object itself is ideal, and Christ is working on it, but he works on it in time. But if you want to think the end of this work, you have to think the end of time, and the end of time is also the end of Christ, because if there were no more time, you could no longer think the difference between Christ and God. The structure, as you can see, is very complex. In truth, Malebranche's real thinking is that this will never happen. He can't say as much, because he's orthodox on this count. But to the extent that he thinks God as subject and being-subject deeply and absolutely, he is well aware: the filling of the hole of God's desire by the ideal object of his completed Church, the perfect mystical body of Christ, is asymptotic and forever on the unreachable horizon.

Let's quickly go back over the stages of this asymptotic labor. Christ thinks of certain things that meet the requirements of his work at a given moment. He is an artist, an architect. When he desires a particular thing, he becomes the occasional cause of grace, and the general law of grace immediately comes into play.

Since the Father never refuses him anything, precisely because this is the law, grace then falls, like the rain, on something that (to us) can seem arbitrary, because *we* are not architects of the work. So it's important to understand that the apparent arbitrariness of grace—the fact that it falls on anyone at all—is ultimately the always-incomplete nature of the work. This incompleteness that we mistake for the arbitrariness of grace is its temporal nature. Christ builds this work through a series of desires that are partial with regard to its perfection. It is therefore an open work into which things come one after the other, in the infinite filling of this opening, which will sometimes require misers, sometimes the righteous, sometimes fanatics, and so on: all the categories of materials Christ is led to think of at a particular moment, with the result that God dispenses grace to them. The effect of grace is to be incorporated into the Church, provided the grace is sufficient. The definition of grace is that grace is related to whether a man desires to be the object of the other's desire, and therefore whether he desires to incorporate himself into the Church.

Christ deals with the demands of his work, a work that is nothing but the service of the Father's desire. These demands make him think at a given moment of a particular thing, whose law is solely the beauty of the Temple, of a particular ornament that is pleasing to his Father. The people who represent this ornament—because the ornaments are souls, after all—will have grace dispensed to them according to a general law, whose author is not Christ. The general law is the law of the simplicity of divine action. So this grace falls on the people in question, but this naturally doesn't mean that it will be sufficient to arouse in them, truly and completely, the desire to be the object of God's desire, for their hearts may in fact be completely hardened. Christ thought of this hardened heart, because he thought it might be good for it to be in the Church, and God let his grace fall. But if this hardened heart did not necessarily become incorporated into the Church, it's because it's a work that, as such, includes Christ's failure. We need to take seriously the fact that it is a work in progress, a temporal construction. It is not for nothing that Malebranche uses the term "materials." Christ handles this material, exactly like an artist who tries something out and comes up against an obstacle: it's not right; he'll have to erase it and try something else. We can easily imagine the incorporation of a large number of misers into the edifice, misers so miserly that even though God had grace fall on them, they still remain just as unsightly and ultimately can't be incorporated into the general edifice. Viewed from this perspective, Christ is God's artist, but he's an artist with his own abilities, which include evoking grace without, however, being master of its effect.

This problem, which is already pretty complicated, will as usual be compounded by Malebranche's acute awareness of the fact that a subjective undertaking or work is subject to obstacles. This is something he accepts, precisely insofar as Christ is not God: sure, he's God, but he's God in his finite disjunction, and therefore subject to obstacles and time. When Christ's wishes are granted by God, they are granted in the sense in which God makes grace fall like the rain, but not in the sense in which God would directly incorporate the people in question into the Church. The problem of grace is that it might not work. There is therefore, from this perspective (if not in the general strategy of desire) a disjunction between God and Christ, and that's what makes it so subtle. Malebranche manages to accommodate the concept of the obstacle, the fascination of the object, the ideal function of time—and, consequently, the true meaning of the work, which is transitive neither to the will nor to the desire of Christ. Otherwise, it would mean that Christ would be God! There will certainly be grace, but it is not certain that grace will be sufficient to ensure the effective incorporation of the intended ornament into the ecclesial Temple.

As architect of the eternal Temple and as God's artist, Christ even maintains a certain indifference to the materials. There will be two cases of this indifference: towards those materials that are not yet incorporated into the Church, the raw materials, the souls that are for the time being totally unconcerned with this matter; and then those who are already incorporated into the Church and who will be called the righteous. Since it's a temporal work, the body of the Church exists at a given moment: these are the people who are already in the Church, whom Christ has thought of, who have already received grace, and for whom, if I can put it this way, grace has worked. For an artist, what is still a raw material is not the same thing as what is already figured or present in the work taking shape. There is what is still formless and what already contributes to the form. So there are two functions, two different statuses. In the first case, Christ is only the architect of the eternal Temple and the materials are chosen in view of the artist's plan: he takes this stone, this color, hence this soul. As Malebranche puts it rather bluntly, concerning the "materials that are not yet part of his Temple, it is indifferent [to Christ] whether he has Paul or John, if one or the other are similar to the idea that determines his desires."[9] Malebranche is well aware that it's an object that causes desire; it's not simply someone, but someone insofar he or she bears an object. If the bearer of the object conforms to what Christ wants to do in given circumstances, it matters little to him whether it's Paul or John, as long as one or the other is similar to the idea that determines his desires. If he wants to incorporate misers and Paul or John are misers, they will do, and it makes no difference whether it is one or the other of them. I already noted this indifference when it came to God.

In the second case of indifference, when the materials are already incorporated, things change, since election and incorporation have already occurred. What happens, Malebranche asks, for those who have followed the movement of grace and been incorporated into the work? What happens for the righteous? Christ has a particular responsibility toward them. It is no longer simply his responsibility as an architect. It is now his role as what Malebranche called "head of the Church." Christ, architect of the eternal Temple, is also head of the Church. This means that he is responsible for the work. He is its first agent. Consequently, when a soul is incorporated into this work, it has a particular status as compared to the soul that is a raw material and about which he doesn't yet know whether he will use it or not to build the Temple. Now, there are righteous men who are condemned, as we see all the time. There are also people who have followed the movements of grace at a given moment and are members of the Church and, then, having succumbed to a temptation, relapse into the status of a castoff. The first interpretation involves the aesthetic. Christ corrects his work; there are erasures—people who were part of it at a certain moment and then are no longer part of it. The righteous man can be tempted, the righteous man can succumb to temptation, the righteous man can become a reprobate, even if he has already been incorporated into the work. Christ is then responsible for this, as head of the Church.

This issue represents a serious problem for Malebranche, who devotes some extremely involved and very fascinating passages to it. How can people who have really been incorporated into the Church nevertheless relapse into sin at some point? How can we be motivated to be part of the Church when we know that this offers us no extra guarantee when it comes to our ultimate destiny? So it's ultimately a political problem, because if belonging to a party brings you no particular guarantee as to your own salvation, you might as well not do anything: grace will fall on you when Christ thinks of you. And if he doesn't think of you any more when you're in the Church than when you aren't, this is very problematic with regard to a matter with which Malebranche is concerned, namely, recruitment—which, as he's well aware, is in danger of drying up.

So he has to reevaluate the situation. Let's reconsider what I said a moment ago. The Church is the body of Christ, not just metaphorically, but in reality, because the Church is really the worldly materiality of God and because all the souls that were won over and incorporated into the Temple constitute the body of Christ down through the ages. A righteous man is part of the mystical body of Christ—he is someone who has followed the movement of grace and has been incorporated alive into the eternal Temple. At this point, Malebranche will compound the problem in the following way: since the righteous are part of the mystical body of Christ, Christ is particularly alert to their needs, by contrast with those who are simple materials. Particularly alert, because it is absolutely important that this concern recruitment. This means that if we are part of the Church and we pray to the intercessor, the mediator, we will be heard. We are not just in the condition of wondering whether Christ, for completely arbitrary (and, for us, impenetrable) reasons, is going to think of us. If he thinks of us as materials, he thinks of us only in view of the project of the work, which we know nothing about, since we have no particular relationship to it. So Malebranche salvages this aspect, which is very important for recruitment, namely that if you are part of the Church, Christ is aware of your needs, of your temptations, of the fact you lack grace at a given moment. Being the head of the Church, he knows the state of mind of its members, each and every one. By contrast, those who are outside the Church might also receive grace, but they will receive it strictly in accordance with God's architectural work. There is therefore a very important difference in status. The relationship to those who are outside the Church is architectonic. It depends on the plans, the aims, and the desires of Christ. The relationship to those who are in the Church is a specific, informed, relationship. The advantage is that this obviously offers something more to the members of the Church. Anyone who is in the Church has a specific relationship with Christ in his role as head of the Church, which is not fused or merged with his role as architect of the eternal Temple. This is beneficial for recruitment, but it compounds the problem even more, because there are nevertheless righteous men who are condemned, even though Christ was aware of their status. And now, it is impossible to use time—the simple series of Christ's desires—as an argument, because, in this case, Christ was immediately aware of their status. Anyone who is part of the Church and prays to Christ is heard. Prayer is efficacious.

This new difficulty will lead Malebranche into some very intricate zigzags, where what is finally at stake is something that must be called the theory of organization, the thinking of organization. Malebranche is very much ahead of his time, a formidable thinker of the Party, in the sense of the communist parties at the time of Stalin. In his thinking there can be found a theory that justifies the endless purges of the party.

Let's take an example. A righteous man is exposed to temptation; since he belongs to the Church, he will pray and ask for grace for himself, so as to be helped through this ordeal. Christ is aware; he is informed of this prayer, of this anguish, of this situation. An unavoidable political point: if we want the Church to have a meaning, then this righteous man can't be abandoned. Informed of the situation, Christ can only desire this man's salvation, since he wants everyone to be saved, since he wants the Temple to be completed. His thought will therefore turn toward this anguish, and he will consequently function as the occasional cause of a grace, automatically. When we are in the Church, our desire for grace is the cause for the occasional cause. Since we are in the Church, Christ will function as the occasional cause. However, as regards those who are not in the Church, he will think of them solely in terms of his undertaking as architect of the Temple. However, there is no getting around the fact that grace will not necessarily be sufficient. There will indeed be a dispensation of grace, but it will not necessarily be enough to prevent some righteous people—who are nevertheless already members of the Party-Church—from succumbing to temptation, whether it be the temptation of sin in the seventeenth century or that of bourgeois ideology in the twentieth.

Malebranche will propose the following theory, which is both farfetched and extremely valuable for better understanding the functioning of the parties of the Third International. In this precise case Christ will in fact intercede with God, but he won't ask God whether the righteous man who is subject to temptation will or will not be saved in accordance with this or that degree of grace. As Malebranche's marvelous phrase has it, Christ, the mediator, "will not be, however, a scrutinizer of hearts."[10] This means that the occasional cause will remain strictly occasional. There was a prayer—that prayer was heard and transmitted—but whether the dispensation of grace associated with this information can rescue the tempted righteous man or not is a question that cannot be Christ's concern. It would concern him only if he added particular knowledge of the situation to his role as occasional cause. In this case, Malebranche will say, "his action would not bear the character of its quality as occasional cause."[11] Here again we can distinguish two underlying lines of thought. At a first level, we can simply say that Christ himself acts in a general way, so that the generality of divine action might be saved. It is clear that Malebranche does not intend to reintroduce through the window what he just sent out the front door: the dispensation of grace is not particular. But it has to be conceded to the people who are part of the Church that they are heard, otherwise it would be hard to understand what the point of being part of the Church would be. But from there to concede to them that they are purely and simply exceptions to the general nature of divine action . . . well, you can see how, little by little, you might be led there. But it is crucial not to make exceptions to the simplicity of divine ways.

There is also a second level, which is very characteristic of the underlying organizational philosophy. In fact, there is no doubt that a real senior official, a head of the Church, or the secretary general of a large party, should know what is going on, should know, for example, that this or that member of his flock is exposed to temptation, that this or that member of the Party has deviant ideas. But on the other hand, being in service to a general work, he should not know too much about it either; he should not burden himself with knowledge that's too specific. He should know what the troubles are, but in such a way that the response he will offer— he must always offer one—will not be too particular, otherwise it could damage the generality of his undertaking. He will therefore intercede in a general way with God (with Stalin?), he will be the occasional cause; there will be grace, but in keeping with the general law. So it is necessary for Christ to preserve a certain amount of ignorance, which is precisely embodied in the fact that he must not be a scrutinizer of hearts. It is important to understand that, in the

Church and the Party alike, there may well be individual situations
(this righteous person or that comrade exposed to such or such a
temptation), but there is strictly speaking no individual. I mean:
there is no individual in the sense that the head of the Church or
the general secretary of the Party would have individual knowledge of this individual. Christ will therefore respond to the anguish
of the righteous man as he would to an individual situation, but
without having to know the individual of this individual situation.
And so the notion of an individual situation is itself a category,
not a singularity. You see this distinction, which is fundamental to
every philosophy of organization. An ignorance, a holy ignorance,
is necessary. What is more, if Christ—or any Party cadre—knew too
much, he could be accused of being wicked, his wickedness consisting in not interceding on the basis of this knowledge. He must subsume the individual under the category of the individual situation,
and not properly speaking under the category of the individual.
When Christ asks that a soul be given grace, he too is in a state of
not-knowing with regard to this soul; there is something unknown
in his action. When he prays for someone in the Church, for a righteous man exposed to temptation—and he does so as soon as he
learns of his anguish—he indeed prays for him, but not absolutely
for *him*: he prays for his situation.

In view of the above, things are even more complicated. It was
immediately objected to Malebranche that, sooner or later, we would
indeed be forced to think that Christ knew everything. Ignorance,
sure—but ultimately, even though Christ's capacity for thought in
the present is finite, its virtual capacity is infinite. Christ, after all,
is God, and every now and again the necessity of the unity of the
three persons in God must be recalled. So Malebranche was blamed
for having founded this whole business on ignorance, whereas, in
the final analysis, there was not ignorance but knowledge. Just as it
could be argued against Stalin that he knew everything about the

members of the Party to whom he ultimately refused any grace and whom he cold-bloodedly allowed to be exterminated.

Whence a final dialectic, which is the following: When Christ intervenes in a situation and not with regard to an individual, it is quite simply because he is not currently thinking of the individual, he is not currently scrutinizing his or her heart. Indeed, his knowledge of the individual is, as a rule, not current. Everyone knows, Malebranche repeats, that $2 + 2 = 4$, but does this mean that we often think of it? The same goes here. Christ may be thoroughly acquainted with an individual's heart, but given the vast quantity of things he has to be concerned with, he does not often think of it. And it is not just because an individual prays to him that he will think of him or her; what he will think of is the intercession, which is immediate since he is the occasional cause. But the upshot is that the enormous quantity of Christ's knowledge, which encompasses everything, is for the most part unconscious, given that the part that is really actualized in the work is minuscule compared with all of that. With God, knowledge is constantly entirely current. With Christ, who is the temporalization of God, the vast quantity of knowledge is in reality unconscious, and only a minuscule amount of it is brought into his consciousness.

I will let you imagine what this argument becomes when applied to Stalinist parties, which I will abandon here to their fate. Anyway, to come back to Malebranche, let's note that it would be completely legitimate to say that Christ is God as unconscious, and that this unconscious of God that Christ really is concerns man—mainly, that is, the object of God's desire. Christ can legitimately be called the unconscious dimension of God's desire, while at the same time he is its actualization, its real. This is what explains phenomena such as the fall of certain righteous people, about which we can say quite simply that it is a symptom. It is the symptomatic aspect of God's desire, related to the fact that Christ is its unconscious dimension.

But what makes Malebranche's thesis unique is that the reason for the unconscious is time, or, in other words, the temporalization of God in the actualization of his desire, which makes Christ a figure of the unconscious itself. This does not mean that Malebranche contradicts Freud's thesis that the unconscious knows no time. Quite the contrary! For the unconscious—the largest part of which is repressed and inaccessible, and very rarely present (this is due to the temporal dimension of Christ's action) —is Christ's total knowledge, that is, eternity, which is only actualizable in eternity, in the eternity of the Father. So in Malebranche's work there is this staggering intuition that time founds the unconscious precisely insofar as the unconscious is itself intemporal and knows no time. And it is with this subtle turn that he will attempt to complete his theory of the subject.

Session 7

May 27, 1986

Our objective today is to conclude this seminar on Malebranche. The question we will be concerned with is the following one: What, ultimately, is Malebranche's doctrine of the human subject?

We have seen—and I'll remind you of it in a few quick theses—that Malebranche undoubtedly has a theory of the divine subject. We've gone over the different figures of this subject. In the framework of this doctrine of the divine subject, humanity—and within humanity, each person—appears in the position of an object, an object that is ultimately the cause of God's desire. So there can be two approaches to our interest in Malebranche. We can say: Malebranche is interesting because there is something paradigmatic about his theory of the divine subject. We can also say: Malebranche thinks a number of things about God that are useful for thinking the human subject, or consistent with what we moderns might think about the human subject.

We can therefore decipher in Malebranche what might be called a macroscopic model of the figure of the subject. This then paves the way for a translation-type exegesis; that is to say, in the final analysis, it's a question of translating Malebranche's theology into terms proper to the modern doctrine of the subject. This is largely what I have done and what has allowed us to see what is at once anticipatory and archaic in his thinking. He is a somewhat ambiguous figure. He is modern in terms of his configuration of categories, since he tries to think being as subject and he maintains unequivocally that the essence of the question of the subject is desire and its structure. That is his properly modern contribution. The archaic aspect is that, when all is said and done, his philosophy appears in the form of a theology. So there is a first approach, which would treat Malebranche as a paradigm or as a macroscopic model, and would assess this enterprise of thought from our modern perspective by showing that there is a sort of anticipation of categories as well as a situational conservatism in Malebranche. The metaphoric aspects remain consistently theological, and so all the enlarging, all the macroscopy, obviously depends on the fact that the subject is God, the object is the world, and the unconscious is Christ.

The other approach, whose aim is to disrupt Malebranche rather than translate him, would interrogate the repercussions of the theological or macroscopic nature of his model of the subject properly speaking, hence of the human subject. It is clear that the macroscopy does not spare Malebranche the microscopy: he still needs to talk about men and the human subject, for after all, it is the latter he is addressing. After all, God can settle his own affairs. He doesn't need a philosopher to enlighten him. He has long enlightened himself, and he enlightened himself to the point of obscuring himself, of incarnating himself, the incarnation being his unconscious figure. Since Malebranche also has to treat the human subject, there will necessarily be symptoms arising from the fact that the matrix of his conception is macroscopic. The question is: What is man if God is a subject? Oddly enough, this is a question that Goetz, the main character of Sartre's play, *The Devil and the Good Lord*, explicitly asks. And not just whether God exists, but whether he exists as a subject, as he does in a radical sense in Malebranche. Goetz's answer is very clear: if God exists as a subject, man does not exist. And Goetz adds that, a contrario, if man exists, God does not exist as a subject. This is exactly what Malebranche's dilemma will be.

How will Malebranche frame the question of man, the question of the human subject, since God is assumed as a subject? Let me recapitulate what I've already said about this. There are two legal orders: the order of nature and the order of grace. If we consider the human subject strictly in the order of nature, we can say that he is in fact a nothing, or so insignificant that he is hardly worth speaking about. It is clear that if by subject we mean the strictly natural subject, which is in reality a natural object, then it is only a null configuration of the scene of God's desire. As pure nature, the human subject is a quasi-nothing—especially since he is not even, strictly speaking, the object of God's desire. What interests God about man is that he should be a member of his Church. However, it is obviously not as a natural body that he can be so; it is as a spiritual being that he is a member of this spiritual body of Christ that is the Church. Consequently, as pure nature, man is not even the object of God's desire. He is at the very most the substructure of the object of such a desire.

If we now consider the human subject in the spiritual order, which is the order of grace, the human subject is the object of God's desire, insofar as he is a member of God's Church and insofar as God desires him to be so. However, we have seen that the human subject could only be a member of the Church if he were touched by grace. That is not enough, though. But it is necessary. What is more, as I have repeatedly stressed, this grace does not concern the human subject as such; it is not sufficient to designate the human subject as singular. From God's point of view, grace does not designate anyone in particular since it is dispensed according to general laws. But then—this is a crucial question—how is the human subject designated in his singularity as a subject, since he isn't designated directly by efficacious grace? As we have seen, the grace of enlightenment, the grace dispensed by God, is dispensed according to general laws of distribution that do not designate him as such, since God, as God, has no particular reason to think of a specific person. God's desire does not single out any person at all. The human subject is certainly the object of God's desire, but what this desire designates is humanity as finitude, in which the infinite incarnates itself, rather than as any singular subject. What eventually singles out a particular subject can only be the occasional cause of grace and the occasional cause of grace is the thought of Christ, the finite thought of Christ. Therefore, strictly speaking, a subject is designated as such, in the spiritual order (the only one that counts), only insofar as Christ thinks of him.

But what is Christ? Christ, as I said, is the making unconscious of divine knowledge, since the conscious part, the currently conscious part, of Christ's thought is finite. It is Christ as God incarnate who thinks of such and such a person and, in so doing, singles him out. Consequently, the infinity of divine knowledge is at all times essentially unconscious in Christ. It is therefore completely legitimate to say that Christ is the making unconscious of divine knowledge, the conscious part being only the tip—which is naturally incommensurable with the latent and inexplicit infinity—of this divine knowledge. As we can see, the singling out of a particular human subject is the way in which the massive unconscious knowledge that God has of men (and here this really means men as multiples of subjective singularities) lets through some conscious figures that have benefited from Christ's attention—an attention that, at a particular moment, falls on such and such a person. In this doctrine, the singling out of the human subject is wholly bound up with the vicissitudes of God's unconscious. One might say: the vicissitudes of his finite consciousness, but his finite conscious mind is only the making unconscious of his true being, of his infinite knowledge. Sticking for the time being to this strict definition of the singling out of the human subject, we can say that to be an object of God's desire means to be subject to chance, to the contingency of God's unconscious. Or again, once God is a subject, being the adequate object of God's desire—the only possible identification of a human subject in this structural framework we are dealing with—ultimately depends on this unconscious of God that Christ is. It is, so to speak, a pure encounter. Christ's thought, the figure of God's unconscious, has encountered such and such a man and in this way he is elected, singled out for God's desire, and therefore in the position of cause of that desire.

When all is said and done, if you ask what Malebranche's doctrine of the unconscious is (of course, this is not his terminology, but as is always the case with him, there is a similar terminology), we could put forward the very interesting thesis that, for him, the unconscious is the infinite structured as something finite. Which allows us to say, in the singular form of the Christian metaphor, that Christ is God's unconscious. Given that the infinite is structured like something finite—not like a language, but like something finite—there is necessarily the unconscious. Now, at this point Malebranche will attempt to turn things around so as to salvage something of the human subject, so as not to reduce it to this aleatory election as object. He will try to define our desire: not God's desire this time, but the human subject's desire. What I'm calling "desire" here he usually calls either "will" or "movement." "Movement" is certainly closer to desire than "will," but in reality, for Malebranche, "movement" and "will" are synonyms, and ultimately it is indeed a question of desire.

So what, for us earthly subjects, is *our* movement, *our* will, *our* desire? We should never lose sight of the general structure, which is that we are, in any event, the adequate objects of God's desire when God's unconscious election has fallen on us. But within this framework, Malebranche tries to elaborate a theory of our desire. The extent to which "desire" here means the same thing it does for God is the whole problem, but it is nevertheless the case that this attempt is a real one. Now, the definition of our desire, of the human subject's desire, will be presented as the exact opposite of God's desire. Our desire—which, as we'll see, also has an unconscious structure—is the finite structured as an infinite. That's the reversal. This means that *our* movement as human subjects, our essential desire, is precisely the desire of God. But "desire *of* God" can mean that our desire is the desire that God has, and therefore that our desire is identical to God's. It can also mean that the object of our desire is God, that we desire God. So there is an ambiguity, and the whole point is that this ambiguity must be maintained as such. The human subject is the desire *of* God, in the double sense that it is the figure of the desire that God has for it, and/or it is a desire whose object is God.

I will now give you a series of statements by Malebranche that establish this attempted reversal. They are all taken from the Third Discourse of the *Treatise on Nature and Grace*, the discourse that specifically concerns the human subject.

The first statement is: "For finally, since God only makes and preserves minds for himself, he carries them towards himself as much as he conserves their being. . . ."[1]

The second statement is: "It [the soul] wills only through the movement which God ceaselessly impresses upon it."[2]

The third statement is: "This natural movement of the soul towards the good in general is invincible, for it does not depend on us to will to be happy."[3]

And finally, the fourth statement is: "All minds love God by the necessity of their nature."[4]

In these four statements, as in many others, we find the ambiguity I mentioned. The human subject's desire is the desire of God. On the one hand, the human subject is desire to the extent that, like every movement, his movement has God as its cause. The movement of the soul is caused by God. As a living process, as a living subject, the spiritual subject is desire, movement, will, and this, in some way, is the effect of divine action. In return, this effect of divine action is a component of God's desire. For, as the first statement says, if God constitutes the human subject at all times as movement or desire, it is ultimately because he himself desires his own glory and, therefore, fundamentally, the being of the human subject is desire, movement, will. In this respect, Malebranche is very similar to Spinoza. But these are finite figures of the desire that God has for himself.

God makes and preserves minds only for himself and therefore, insofar as he preserves their being, he preserves their desiring sense. It is indeed true that the human subject—human desire—is God's desire in the ontological sense, that is, in the sense of an overlapping in being between human desire and the desire God has for himself. This is the first side of the issue.

The other side, which is absolutely inseparable from the first, is that, as a result, God is also the object of human desire. This is what the third and fourth statements say. Seen from without, that is, considered in the context of ontology, human desire is part of the desire that God has for his own glory, and it is from this that it derives its whole being. But seen from within, or subjectively—or again from the point of the view of the finite itself—what is given is the desire *for* God, this time in the sense that God is its object. This desire is invincible and indestructible. Furthermore, God carries minds toward himself as much as he preserves their being; thus, our being, our subjective being, is rigorously coextensive with the desire we have for God. This desire is just as indestructible as our being and it structures our whole life. Only death puts an end to it, by opening us up to a transfiguration of another sort. But let's stick with earthly life. Bear in mind that this indestructibility of finite desire, which is our soul, derives from the fact that its sole cause is the infinite, i.e., God himself. That's naturally why the movement of the soul toward the good in general is invincible. Ultimately, finite desire is structured by the infinite in the ambiguity of the maxim "human desire is the desire of God," where God is at once in the position of being and in the position of object. We could therefore define the human subject by the fact that it is the desire of God. And since it is the anthropological figure, the subjective figure, that interests us, we will effectively take God as the object of this desire and we will say that man is the finite being who desires the infinite. Desiring should be understood in the narrowest sense of the term, namely, in the sense in which the infinite is the object, the cause, of desire.

Once we concede this point, which is consistent with the presuppositions, there are still two significant problems. The first problem: it is not at all obvious, empirically and anthropologically, that man is this being who desires God. Some people attest to that fact, others don't. Why is it that most of the time we don't know whether they do or not? The second problem now, which is not a new one: If it is of the essence of human desire to desire God, why are there damned people, reprobates? Some people were deprived of the Church. Now, to be a part of the Church is precisely to be in the desire *of* God, in the double sense of this phrase. It is important to understand that people deprived of the Church are deprived of their own desire. As is his wont, Malebranche compounds the problem here, by positing that it is of the inner and essential structure of the human subject to desire God. If there are reprobates, it's because they have been deprived of their own desire; they are unaware of their own desire. The problem is all the greater in that Malebranche has said that this desire was invincible. The movement of the soul toward the good in general—but the good in general is God—is invincible. A reprobate is therefore an oxymoron: a defeated invincibility.

What it means to be deprived of one's own desire is a very important problem. Psychoanalysis has recognized this indestructibility and invincibility of desire. As we know, this hardly prevents misfortune and disorientation any more than, in Malebranche, it precludes man's fall or damnation. So it's a crucial problem. To clarify this point, there will obviously need to be a theory of repression, a theory of object substitution. The structure of ignorance of our own desire consists in the fact that something other than God can nevertheless be regarded as the object of this desire, even though it is of the essence of this desire to have God as its object. Something can metaphorize God, that is, make him drop into the unconscious, transform him into the unconscious object of our desire, while a substitute rules over our conscious soul. This theory of object substitution is explicit in Malebranche, and he calls this singular object, which metaphorically replaces the real object of desire, which is always God, "a particular good." A particular good can substitute for the general good, which is God. Or a finite good, a finite object, can be the metaphor of the infinite object. What happens then is actually that my desire of God is unconscious. It falls into the position of being the unconscious truth of my desire for some particular finite object. And this, says Malebranche, is what happens—he doesn't say "unconsciously," that's not his word—every time a particular good is substituted for the general good. A finite object metaphorizes the infinite object, and my unconscious desire—my desire for God, which is the structure of my being—drops into the unconscious.

Let's make sure we understand this. For Malebranche, if I desire a woman, this woman is always a metaphor for God. All concupiscence is metaphorical. It's not the case, strictly speaking, that I've preferred concupiscence to the love of God. Malebranche's vision is much too subtle for it to be reduced to assuming that there are general systems of possible desires, among which we find lofty and sublime desires, such as the desire for God, and, on the other hand, low and vulgar desires, like concupiscence. There is only one desire, which is the desire for God, and there is only one object, which can be metaphorized. Consequently, concupiscent desire is the same as the desire for God. The focus on the object can be errant or metaphorical, but not the desire itself.

So in Malebranche's work there is this absolutely extraordinary thesis to the effect that the most abominable sins are only metaphors of the desire for God. A very convincing thesis, in my opinion, and much more insightful than the distinction between high and low parts of the subject, or than Plato's tripartition of the soul, or than those hierarchical structures by which we supposedly control the lower concupiscent desires by higher faculties. It is at once more radical and more convincing. That said, what proves that it's a metaphor? Because if nothing proves that it is, then any cure for it is impossible. We might even be led to think that, after all (since it is the desire for God that is expressed in this way), everything's fine. Does it really matter whether the invincible desire for God is metaphorized as a woman, the thirst for power, or things of that sort?

In fact, there is nevertheless a symptom that indicates that it's metaphorical. A desire is a desire for a metaphorical object when it turns out, in a field of experience to be defined—but which, for example, the confessor is able to verify by his own action—that the desire for a particular object, however strong that desire may be, is not, strictly speaking, invincible. What is especially interesting here is that what is a symptom for Malebranche's subject is not the compulsive and automatic nature of the desire, its apparent invincibility, but the consciousness of its precariousness. This desire can be very powerful, but it's possible to confirm that the truth of its nature, seemingly compulsive and obligatory, is that it's actually precarious and terminable. Unconscious desire, which is in fact the correlation of the living subject with the infinite object, is invincible. The desire for the finite object is the same: there are not two different desires. The change in object is not a change in desire. Something of its essential attribute has simply remained unconscious, namely, its invincibility, which remains a predicate attached to the desire for the infinite object. What drops out is therefore not the desire itself but its invincibility. In the case of the finite object the desire is the same, but the predicate of invincibility is in some way withdrawn from it. The cure then consists in bringing both the invincibility and the infinite object back to the surface. If you manage to switch the position of the object in such a way that the infinite object returns to its place, you will have the invincibility back as well, and you will have a subject who is genuinely cured. The problem is obviously how to bring about this switching of objects.

This will produce a unique theory of what Malebranche calls "freedom." Freedom results from the fact that the desire for the metaphorical object is not invincible and that the desire is no longer invincible once its object is a substitute object. As Malebranche puts it, in very telling fashion: "this expression, *our will is free*, signifies that the natural movement of the soul towards the good in general, is not invincible with respect to the good in particular."[5] Despite its apparent simplicity, this is in fact an extremely complicated formulation, because Malebranche takes special care not to split up desire. He does not say that the movement of the soul toward the good in general is invincible, whereas the movement of the soul toward the good in particular wouldn't be. He says that the natural movement toward the good in general, which is the only movement, ceases to be invincible when its object becomes a particular good. What is in question here is therefore solely the change in object, and not the desire itself. Consequently, the human subject as desiring subject is essentially a subject whose desire—which is always desire for the infinite—is captured in a finite metaphor. Being captured in the finite metaphor defeats invincibility, or abandons it to the unconscious. As a result, invincibility becomes an attribute of the unconscious and for that very reason the conscious mind is free with regard to metaphors. As a result—and this is very important—the pull exerted by the substitute object, the force of attraction that makes us desire a particular fetish instead of desiring God, does not lie in the desire itself. For the desire in its being, in its inner essence, is the desire for God, and the object itself can add no particular force to it. In reality, it can only strip it of its invincibility.

So we are forced to ask where this pervasiveness of metaphor comes from, and why it is that, despite everything, most men revel in metaphor. Here too, we'll encounter Malebranche's method of compounding problems. If desire is really invincible only as the desire for God, if the desire for the substitute, finite object is not itself invincible, why is it that the human subject—men in general— are nevertheless so strongly attached to these metaphors, to such an extent that a therapeutic war, which mobilizes religious orders and countless confessionals, etc., needs to be waged in order to combat this metaphorical invasion? Malebranche has a really fascinating theory on this subject, which is that the power of the metaphor, the power of the metaphorical object, is not in desire as movement. We know that desire as movement is strongest precisely when the object is the divine, infinite object and that, insofar as we have a genuine repetition compulsion, it concerns God. The only thing that is really invincible, compulsive, endlessly repetitive, is the love of God. The rest is caught up in the vicissitudes of non-invincibility. But that's not the source of the metaphorical object's power. Its power comes from something completely different: pleasure, which Malebranche explicitly says is pleasure as rest, that is, as the suspension of desire. The infinite good has the disadvantage of making us desire endlessly. The finitude of the metaphorical object draws its charm not from the fact that we desire the object (though it is undeniable that we do), but from its ability to suspend desire. This is the definition of pleasure, which Malebranche expresses in this way: "the soul ordinarily rests as soon as it has found some good: it stops at it to enjoy it."[6] This means that the substitute object, the "placeholder" for God—for every object is a placeholder for God—draws its power as the cause of desire from the fact that it is the metaphorical cause of its suspension. Its superiority over God is not of the order of desire, but of the order of rest. As the cause of the suspension, it is not metaphorical, naturally. But insofar as it comes, as a metaphor, into position as the cause of desire, it has the additional virtue of suspending desire, of bestowing it as pleasure. Of course, this only lasts for a short time. We rest, and then desire starts up again. Malebranche is well aware of this. And a new object will come as a substitute, which will once again bring us rest, and then the cycle starts over again, so that man is always in the state of a wanderer, in Malebranche's view. Man is the Don Juan not of women but of the finite metaphors of God.

Malebranche says next to nothing about women (save in always very cautious terms) with regard to the marriage of Christ and his Church, albeit always interpreting it as a metaphor, because he is much more interested in the Church as the body than as the bride of Christ. Moreover, it was not appropriate for an Oratorian priest to seem to be too knowledgeable about such things. That said, it must be acknowledged that his descriptions are strikingly reminiscent of the description of Don Juanism. In these paragraphs that Malebranche, that Baroque aesthetician, devotes to this question there is the thread of an already pre-Romantic theme: that of the endless pursuit, of forever-unsatisfied desire, of rest that is always only temporary, of the halt on the path of life, and so on. This metaphor of the state of the wanderer—this kind of figure of wandering from one substitute object to another—is quite odd. It has to do, of course, with someone whose life (as Malebranche will moreover say) is given over to concupiscence. So it's really the libertine who is in question. But this libertine is nevertheless romanticized, because Malebranche is held back by the fact that, ultimately, it is God whom this metaphorical desiring desires. Even if the libertine—instead of having the invincibility of the desire for God—has taken up residence in the restful and constantly suspended precariousness of the desire for the object, he still has a desire for God. Male-branche must condemn him, however, and he does. But we sense that, in the conception he has of it, the state of being a wanderer is a real figure of the human subject for him, including in the structure of the desire for God.

Now that the general structure of the human subject's desire has been reconstructed this way, the question we must still address is how grace comes into the picture. Because we've left grace a little aside. After all, the spiritual subject, the soul, belongs to the order of grace. How does grace act on a subject thus constituted? That's the problem. Up to this point, when I spoke about grace, I assumed that it acted. But how will it act on the human desiring subject defined in this way? It will not do so purely and simply through the intervention of the infinite, real object. Malebranche is much too knowledgeable about the figures of the subject to think such utter nonsense. He knows full well that what might be effective on a subject fallen prey to metaphor cannot be a pure and simple reversal of the situation, which would in fact be a particular miracle. Now, if there are general laws for the distribution of grace, they should be consistent with the structure of human desire, and there is no question of shoving desire's real object, on a case-by-case basis, in the subject's face, as a brutal analyst might do. Malebranche is too subtle for that. But it cannot be a new metaphor either, a different, more appropriate finite object, for example. We could imagine that sublime objects might be substituted for an object of luxury, ambition, sordid greed, gold, a woman, and so on. But Malebranche is not a fan of sublimation either. So it's neither one nor the other, and this "neither . . . nor" can often be found in his work, because he has a very subtle mind: it's neither the brutality of the real object summoned back arbitrarily, nor a sublimated, or sublime, object.

The grace brought about by Christ will act by dispensing a pleasure with no representable cause, a pleasure with no object. Theology and Malebranche call this objectless pleasure a "prevenient delectation." It is miraculous. It's also called "the grace of feeling." This prevenient delectation will counterbalance the force of the metaphorical cause, which, I remind you, is pleasure—that is, suspension. It will mean for us that there is a rest with no object, that is, a pleasure of desire as such, of desire with no object, with no representable object. Now, desire as such goes toward God. Not to have an object is strictly equivalent to being reduced to its being, and its being corresponds to God. Ultimately, the pleasure of desire as such is the pleasure of God. So we can say that the prevenient delectation, the grace of feeling, suspends the metaphorical suspension by using the same weapons it does, but by arousing a pleasure with no object. Malebranche touches upon a very important issue here, whose literary fate has been remarkable. We need only think of Rousseau's *Rêveries*, in which Rousseau tries to define what a pleasure with no object might be, or of all the later attempts to apprehend the superiority, in terms of pleasure, of desire over pleasure. It is on this that Malebranche focuses with great skill. It is in this prevenient delectation that we find the action of Christ. At the moment when we are tempted to linger in a concupiscient rest, the prevenient delectation reminds us that desire as such is sufficient, and that the object is superfluous. We can equate prevenient delectation with a destitution of metaphors. As such, it is therefore invincible and brings back invincibility, since it suspends the metaphorical object. It is invincible with the invincibility of desire itself to the extent that, by destituting metaphor, it summons up desire as such, desire that is, as we know, invincible.

Naturally, the result is that there is no merit in renouncing concupiscence through prevenient delectation. We have simply been summoned to the invincibility of the desire for the real object through the suspension and destitution of the metaphor. This is a major problem for Malebranche, because the question of merit is a

real question. We know very well that saving moral merit is required
for the Church. Otherwise, one can always say: "I'm waiting for prevenient delectation—but while I'm waiting, hooray for metaphors!
Let's see what happens!" No, a doctrine of merit is absolutely necessary. And here, we naturally find ourselves at an impasse. The moral
merit without which all preaching—to the extent that it purports
to be militant—ultimately proves to be futile necessarily consists in
desiring God, but in desiring him more than the prevenient delectation requires us to. Because you can well understand that if it's a
pleasure that is superior to all others, then there's not much merit
involved. Now, prevenient delectation, I must stress, is a pleasure.
It's a pleasure with no object, but a pleasure nonetheless. You might
think that someone who gives in to prevenient delectation has
merit because he or she has become better than someone else, but
in fact the question of whether one is better is absolutely different from whether or not one has merit. Because as long as being
better results from the invincibility of prevenient delectation, you
yourself have nothing to do with it. Especially since the laws of the
distribution of grace are entirely different from the internal logic
of the subject as such. We must absolutely not fall back on the idea
of the unconscious election by God. That would hardly sit well with
someone who preaches in the hope of rallying new believers to the
Church, nor with someone who wants to avoid pure and simple
predestination.

So we see that this question is quite complicated. We know that
the substitute metaphor, that is, the object of concupiscence, is in
a position of non-invincibility vis-à-vis God. So we either abandon ourselves to this non-invincibility and it is suspended by prevenient delectation, or, using resources coming from something
else—from what, though, is the whole problem—we do not abandon ourselves to it, without the prevenient delectation, which is
invincible. So this means without grace, since God hasn't willed

anything with regard to a particular subject. It is therefore without grace or without sufficient grace, or with a brief and incomplete prevenient delectation, etc. We must never lose sight of the general horizon of things. In Malebranche's theological setup grace is dispensed without regard for the particular conditions of the sinner or of the finite subject. It is dispensed according to general laws, which themselves refer to God's general project in the creation of the world, which is focused exclusively on the establishment of his Church. Consequently, it is not logically impossible for someone to desire God for reasons that, in their own order, exceed what the grace dispensed requires.

If we tighten things up quite a bit, the fact that God might dispense insufficient grace may seem unbearable. But the fact that sufficient grace does not suffice leads, in the exploration of what that means exactly, to various dialectics that are far more interesting than maintaining that, by definition, sufficient grace suffices. Malebranche does not have a doctrine of sufficient grace; he has no trouble admitting that graces dispensed, whether they are those of enlightenment or those of feeling (since that is his distinction) can be insufficient. He never said that a grace dispensed was necessarily a sufficient grace. It is precisely in the case where grace is insufficient with regard to the difficulty of the situation—for example, with regard to the weight of the temptation concerned—that the question of the possible "extra" with regard to grace comes into the picture. It's important to understand that we are not dealing with a logic in which salvation in its entirety depends exclusively on the sufficiency of grace. In Malebranche's general theological corpus, he tries to claim that there is an order of grace related to the fact that, ultimately, God wants to save all men. Then, he deals with the question of sinners and reprobates, in an order that ultimately refers to what he himself has proposed as a specific doctrine on the subject: given God's plans, grace cannot be dispensed according to particular situations. There is a general order of the dispensation of grace whereby it falls like the rain, as much on the sea or on the desert sands as on fertile land.

I am not saying that, from this point of view, Malebranche will truly get around the question of the "extra something" that the prevenient delectation represents. But it is a valid question, in its own order. He calls it the question of "merit." The question of merit, Malebranche will say, is one of desiring God more than prevenient delectation requires us to, because prevenient delectation is in fact invincible. Merit, if it exists, is something that is in excess over the suspension of the suspension, something that is not simply caught up in the balance between metaphoric pleasure and pleasure with no object, because the action of the prevenient delectation is the counterbalancing of the pleasure with no object by the pleasure that comes from the metaphorical object. Where can this merit come from? From the idea that God is truly our good, hence the real object coming into position as the object, which Malebranche formulates in the following terms: "When the mind sees clearly by the light of reason that God is its good . . ."[7] The difference between the prevenient delectation's mode of effect and the mode I'm speaking of here is only that, in this case, there is a destitution of the metaphorical object by the prevenient delectation—in other words, there is a pleasure with no object, and if there is pleasure with no object, it is the pleasure of desire itself, since the very being of desire is to be the desire for God. But this doesn't mean that with the prevenient delectation the infinite object is represented. It is very important to understand that the efficacy of the prevenient delectation is suspensive and not representative. That's why it's really a question of a grace "of feeling." Malebranche will even use the term "instinct" in this connection. The sole "extra something " possible is that the object be represented, that the infinite object actually appear, consciously, as the object of desire. In other words, that there no longer be any metaphor. Not that the object of desire be destituted, but that there no longer be any metaphor: that is, that there be, in addition to the suspension of metaphorical objects, to which the prevenient delectation gives invincible force, the advent of the good object.

That's what merit is. Merit is defined axiomatically, like everything in Malebranche. Merit is what structures my desire as desire for God, beyond the prevenient delectation. This is what makes the real object come into representation. We have an idea of the infinite. The infinite is thinkable, representable. This has been the case since Descartes. But the problem is that Malebranche will name the representative function "reason." So, if we strip "merit" of its intuitive connotation, we can say that every time the real object of desire is presented—and it is only presentable to thought—there is an excess over the simple suspensive efficacy of the prevenient delectation. Merit is quite simply an extra something in relation to the suspensive effect of the prevenient delectation. What is presupposed is that the infinite as thought, that is, the thought of the infinite, amounts to the same thing as the infinite as object of desire; that the thought of God, the thought of the infinite, is equivalent to the position of the infinite as object of desire, as cause of desire. This is obviously not faithful to the fact that Malebranche thinks the subject as desire, because the fact that the infinite might be thinkable, the fact that I might think (this is why he speaks of reason) that God is my good, does not place God effectively in the position of object of my desire. These two things are absolutely different. In other words, the subtle turn is that the thought of God is the thought of God as object, i.e., that it is the effective representation of the original object. Which, if you think about it, amounts to saying that the thought of God ultimately amounts to the desire for desire.

On a less speculative level, leaving aside the identification of formal contradictions (which is not our primary objective here), I think the veritable sticking point is the following: what Malebranche sidesteps, in fact, and where he is most profoundly opposed to Pascal, is that every desiring eruption of the original object is signaled not by thought but by anxiety. In certain respects, Malebranche's philosophy, with its extreme sophistication and its constant cunning, its successive circumventions, its compounding of problems and resolutions by means of counterbalances, is largely a philosophy that wants to do without anxiety, that wants to de-existentialize the question of God, whereas for Pascal, as we know, anxiety is a central experience. In my own terms, from the point of view of the systematization of the subject, here's what I would say: The crucial experience of the excess of the real, whatever its nature, is effectively anxiety, as Freud and Lacan have shown. What saves us, accordingly, is not reason but courage. And if we define courage—as I have always done—as the process of subjectivation that is at the very point of anxiety, that is the transmutation of anxiety, and whose object is the same, we inevitably come across the essential element of the wager precisely because the experience of the excess of real is anxiety, and anxiety can only be surmounted by a courageous wager. Pascal is also well aware that what is crucial is the undecidable couple of anxiety and courage, while Malebranche is someone who excises this dimension, this couple, and who organizes the whole of his conceptualization solely around the parameters of justice and the superego. For him, justice is the simplicity of ways, the transparency of the divine project, the balanced and ornamented Temple: what he calls divine Wisdom. As for the superego, which is the same thing but on its other face, we have no choice but to acknowledge God's sadism in it. Whatever way you look at it, whatever way Malebranche colors its figure for us, we always encounter the terrifying nature of his God, whose plan, whatever the marginal ornamentations, appears as a completely narcissistic one, of which we are the instruments.

I would not hesitate to argue that Malebranche, in his way, proposes a remarkable theory of the subject to us, but a theory of what

I would call a "half-subject," a subject reduced to its architectonic parameters, a subject that I would call "dis-tressed," if you accept, as I've proposed, that the subject is what develops in the "tress" of four concepts: anxiety, courage, justice, and superego. And deep down we understand why, with regard to these questions of the subject, grace, and Christian modernity—which amount to asking what a Christian subject is after the scientific revolution, a subject of the Galilean era, of the post-Cartesian era—the core conflict, which is not truly a conflict but rather an opposition, is the confrontation between Malebranche and Pascal. It can be said that, for Pascal, there is virtually a complete complement of subjective operators, with a dark coloration, most likely, which comes from the prevalence of the anxiety-superego couple. But there is the crucial element of completeness, the wager, which is to say the acute consciousness of the connection between subject and undecidable, the modern connection between subject and undecidable: impossible for God to be, impossible for him not to be. The wager has to be made between two real impossibilities, whereas in Malebranche we find a peerless architecture based on the architectonic parameters of justice and the superego. But we also find, through constant restorations of successive balances—up to the moment when it becomes too precarious—a sort of evasion, a way of avoiding the mirror-imaging of divine justice and its opposite, namely, the atrocity it represents, its ultimately criminal character. From this point of view, the philosophy of Malebranche appears as a long project of absolution. How can God be absolved? How can we absolve God for having created us for his glory, solely for his glory? I think that, beyond the eighteenth century and the relative withering away of these controversies, the ultimate modernity, as to the question of the Christian subject, is Pascal's. Which allows us to explain Malebranche's always ultimately minor status, despite the great anticipations his work contains. The clear successor to this Pascalian source would no doubt be Kierkegaard, insofar as he asks, at the beginning of the nineteenth century, what a Christian subject is after Hegel, just as the others had asked what a Christian subject was after Descartes. In so doing, Kierkegaard would come back in close contact with the Pascalian dynamic, and would write the most remarkable philosophical text on anxiety.

If we want to offer a balanced judgment of Malebranche, we can say that his great power lies in his capacity for analytical anticipation (in the purely conceptual sense of the term). His need for sophisticated counterbalancing, based on an ultimately radical hypothesis—being is subject—leads him to subtle, rich, and useful analytical connections, but somehow the meaning is missing. In this indisputable analytic virtuosity, something of the meaning is lacking. This is why we can sometimes see in Malebranche an anticipation on the question of the subject—analytical, conceptual, categorial— and at other times a desperate attempt at conservation. Whereas, finally, Pascal, as Christian as he is, is not a conservative, any more than Kierkegaard is. And so what happened to Malebranche was what his ontological aesthetic basically foreshadowed: he became a bit like a monument you visit, saying "What incredible details, how astonishing it is, what luminous stained glass windows!" But it is a monument for which there is no use other than visiting and admiring it, or attempting fragmentary uses of its ornaments. And, borrowing his metaphor of the temple and its ornaments, we might say that he succumbed to his own categories. He was not someone who saved the Church, but someone who built an intellectual monument to it. So he, too, built a Church, but a Church that probably had no services.

Notes

Editors' Introduction to the English Edition of the Seminars of Alain Badiou

1. On October 19, 2015, in a session from his final seminar on "The Immanence of Truths," Badiou describes two distinct but equivalent paths of entry into his work: the first "systematic approach" involves reading, preferably in order, his three or four great works (depending on whether one counts *Theory of the Subject* as part of that sequence or as the prelude to a trilogy). The second "methodical" but not systematic path [*le voyage ordonné*] involves beginning with his *Manifesto for Philosophy* and *Second Manifesto for Philosophy*, to establish the fundamental structure, ligatures, and knots of his thought, followed by, in no particular order, the seminars—now expected to extend to twenty volumes.

Introduction to the Seminar on Malebranche

1. Nicolas Malebranche, *Treatise on Nature and Grace*, trans. with an introduction and notes by Patrick Riley (Oxford: Clarendon Press, 1992). [All notes are the translator's.]
2. Alain Badiou, *L'Un. Descartes, Kant, Platon. 1983–1984* (Paris: Fayard, 2016).
3. Alain Badiou, *The Seminar: Lacan (Antiphilosophy 3), 1994–1995*, trans. Susan Spitzer and Kenneth Reinhard and introduction by Kenneth Reinhard (New York: Columbia University Press, 2018).
4. Alain Badiou, *Parménide. L'être 1—Figure ontologique. 1985–1986* (Paris: Fayard, 2014).
5. Alain Badiou, *Heidegger. L'être 3—Figure du retrait. 1986–1987* (Paris: Fayard, 2015).

6. Alain Badiou. *L'Infini. Aristote, Spinoza, Hegel. 1984–1985* (Paris: Fayard, 2016).

7. Alain Badiou, *Theory of the Subject*, trans. Bruno Bosteels (London: Continuum, 2009); Alain Badiou, *Being and Event*, trans. Oliver Feltham (London: Continuum, 2005).

8. See, for example, *Being and Event*, 149: "This infinity—once subtracted from the empire of the one, and therefore in default of any ontology of Presence—proliferates beyond everything tolerated by representation, and designates—by a memorable inversion of the anterior age of thought—the finite itself as being the exception."

9. Gilles Deleuze, *The Fold: Leibniz and the Baroque*, trans. Tom Conley (Minneapolis: University of Minnesota Press, 1992). Badiou composed a long review article on Deleuze's book, now collected in Alain Badiou, *The Adventure of French Philosophy*, trans. Bruno Bosteels (London: Verso, 2012), 241–68. Badiou devoted an important chapter to Leibniz and the "indiscernible" in his *Being and Event*, 315–23.

10. Alain Badiou, *Parménide*, 8.

11. See *The Adventure of French Philosophy*, in particular the essays "The Fascism of the Potato" and "An Angel has Passed."

12. Bruno Bosteels has written extensively and insightfully on Badiou's work produced between 1969 and 1982, and remains the foremost authority on this period of Badiou's thought.

13. Badiou, *Being and Event*, 212.

14. Malebranche, *Treatise on Nature and Grace*, Discourse 1, 112. Henceforward cited as *TNG*.

15. This expression will play a key role in *Being and Event*'s conceptuality. See *Being and Event*, 175ff.

16. Malebranche, *Traité de la nature et de la grâce*, Discourse 2.17, "Addition," in *Oeuvres complètes*, vol. 2, ed. Antoine-Eugène Genoude and Henri de Lourdoueix (Paris: Sapia, 1837), 319.

17. *TNG*, Discourse 2.17, 144.

18. Alain Badiou, *Ethics: An Essay on the Understanding of Evil*, trans. Peter Hallward (London: Verso, 2001), 48.

About the 1986 Seminar on Malebranche

1. Alain Badiou, *Le Séminaire, l'Un. Descartes, Platon, Kant. 1983–1984* (Paris: Fayard, 2016). [All notes are those of the translator.]

2. Alain Badiou, *Le Séminaire, Parménide. L'être I—Figure ontologique. 1985–1986* (Paris: Fayard, 2014).

3. Alain Badiou, *Le Séminaire, Heidegger. L'être 3—Figure du retrait. 1986–1987* (Paris: Fayard, 2014).

4. Martial Gueroult. *Malebranche* (Paris: Aubier-Montaigne, 1955–59), 3 vols.

Session 1

1. Nicolas Malebranche, *The Search After Truth*, ed. and trans. Thomas M. Lennon and Paul J. Olscamp (Cambridge: Cambridge University Press, 1997).

2. Malebranche, *The Search After Truth*, 115–17.

3. Blaise Pascal, *Pensées*, ed. and trans. Roger Ariew (Indianapolis, IN: Hackett, 2004), 133.

4. Yves Marie André, *La vie du R. P. Malebranche, prêtre de l'Oratoire: avec l'histoire de ses ouvrages* (Geneva: Slatkine reprints, 1970).

5. All references to Malebranche's works in French will be to Nicolas Malebranche, *Oeuvres completes de Malebranche*, 2 vols., ed. Antoine-Eugène Genoude and Henri de Lourdoueix (Paris: Sapia, 1837).

6. Malebranche, Discourse 1.1, in *Treatise on Nature and Grace*, trans. with an introduction and notes by Patrick Riley (Oxford: Clarendon Press, 1992), 112.

7. Martial Guéroult, *Malebranche*, 3 vols. (Paris: Aubier, 1955–59).

Session 2

1. Malebranche, *Traité de la nature et de la grâce*, Discours 2.17, "Addition," in *Oeuvres complètes*, 2 vols., ed. Antoine-Eugène Genoude and Henri de Lourdoueix (Paris: Sapia, 1837), 2:319.

2. Malebranche, *Treatise on Nature and Grace*, trans. Patrick Riley (Oxford: Clarendon, 1992), Discourse 2.55, 164.

3. This passage from Bossuet's "Oraison funèbre de Marie-Thérèse" is cited and translated by Patrick Riley in his "Introduction" to *Treatise on Nature and Grace*, 70.

4. Madame de Sévigné, *Lettres*, tome 2, ed. Emile Gérard-Gailly (Paris: Gallimard, 1960), 798 [my translation].

5. Badiou here paraphrases the first proposition of Malebranche's *Treatise on Nature and Grace*: "God ... cannot have had any other plan in the creation of the world than the establishment of his Church," *TNG*, Discourse 1.1, 112.

Session 3

1. Nicolas Malebranche, *Oeuvres complètes*, tome 2, ed. Antoine-Eugène Genoude and Henri de Lourdoueix (Paris: Sapia, 1837), 297. These lines are drawn from an "addition" to the "Avertissement" to Malebranche's *Treatise* that is not reproduced in Patrick Riley's English translation.
2. Malebranche, *Treatise on Nature and Grace*, trans. with an introduction and notes by Patrick Riley (Oxford: Clarendon Press, 1992), Discourse 1.1, 112. Hereafter cited as *TNG*.
3. *TNG*, Discourse 1.13, 116.
4. *TNG*, Discourse 1.14, 116.
5. *TNG*, Discourse 1.14, 116.
6. *TNG*, Discourse 1.22, 119–20.
7. *TNG*, Discourse 1.2, 112.
8. Malebranche, *Oeuvres complètes*, Discours 1.1, "Addition," 2:297.
9. Discours 1.1, 2:297.
10. Discours 1.1, 2:297.
11. Discours 1.1, 2:299.
12. Discours 1.1, 2:299.

Session 4

1. *TNG*, Discourse 1,3, "Addition"; *Oeuvres complètes*, 2:299.
2. *TNG*, Discourse 1.3, "Addition"; Discours 1.3, 2:299.
3. Discours 1.3, 2:305: "God has but two laws: order, which is his inviolable law . . ." [my translation]. This remark is found in the "Addition" to *Treatise* 1.20, not included in the published English version of the text.

Session 5

1. *TNG*, Discourse 1.24, 121.
2. *TNG*, Discourse 2.8, 141.
3. *TNG*, Discourse 1.30, 124.
4. *TNG*, Discourse 1.37, 126.
5. Discourse 1.38, "Addition"; *Oeuvres complètes*, 2: 309.
6. Discourse 1.39, "Addition"; *Oeuvres complètes*, 2: 309.
7. *TNG*, Discourse 1.41, 128. [Only the phrase "Dieu défait et refait sans cesse" appears in the English translation—Tr.]
8. *TNG*, Discourse 1.44, 129–30.
9. *TNG*, Discourse 2.6, 140–41.

Session 6

1. *TNG,* Discourse 2.4, 140.
2. Ibid.
3. *TNG,* Discourse 2.6, 140.
4. *TNG,* Discourse 2.11, 142.
5. Ibid.
6. Ibid.
7. *TNG,* Discourse 2.17, 144.
8. *TNG,* Discourse 2.16, 144.
9. *TNG,* Discourse 2.17, "Addition," *Oeuvres complètes,* 2:319.
10. *TNG,* Discourse 2.17, "Addition," *Oeuvres complètes,* 2:322.
11. Ibid.

Session 7

1. *TNG,* Discourse 3.1, 169–70.
2. Ibid.
3. *TNG,* Discourse 3.2, 170.
4. Ibid.
5. *TNG,* Discourse 3.3, 170.
6. *TNG,* Discourse 3.8, 173.
7. *TNG,* Discourse 3.24, 184.

Index

absolute singularity, 24

absolution, 175

absurdity, 36

Adam, 75, 78

aesthetics, 143; aesthetic ontology, 70, 82, 115, 117, 131, 176; aesthetic perfection, 72; aesthetic pleasure, 84, 87; of Being, 69; of grace, 84, 122; of nature, 119; of salvation, 84; simplicity of ways, aesthetic law of, 97

Ahmed Gets Angry (Badiou), xv

Ahmed the Philosopher (Badiou), xv

Ahmed the Subtle (Badiou), xv

antinatural acts, 57

L'antiphilosophie 1. Nietzsche (seminar), 195

L'antiphilosophie 2. Wittgenstein (seminar), 195

L'antiphilosophie 3. Lacan (seminar), 195

L'antiphilosophie 4. Saint Paul (seminar), 195

anxiety, 174, 175

architectonic philosophy, 30, 53, 85

Aristotle, xxii, 106

Arnauld, Antoine, xxv, xxvi, 14, 16, 44; career of, 43; flight to Holland

by, 45; in Jansenist party, 38; Malebranche and, 39, 41, 47; *The Search After Truth* and, 18; *Treatise on Nature and Grace* and, 46

astrology, 132

atheism, 39, 62

Aubervilliers, xv, xvi

Augustine (Saint), 1, 48, 49

autonomy, 90

axioms of Malebranche, 22, 52, 56

balancing concepts, 27

balancing resolution of problems, 74

Baroque, xxiii; artist God, 83, 92; Baroque appearance of Malebranche's philosophy, 85, 87; desire and, 142; experimental, 22

beauty, xxx, 83, 105

Beckett et Mallarmé (seminar), 195

Being, xxii; aesthetics of, 69; as calculating subject, 65; generously distributed, 83; history of, xxxvi; as innate, 35; intelligibility of, xxxvi; Malebranchian doctrine of, 24; modes of, 20; non-being, 69, 70, 82; nothingness and, 89, 103, 139, 140;

Being (*continued*)
    ontological figure of, xxii; other-
    than-being, 91; Pascal and, xxviii;
    proliferation of being under
    ontological laws, 23; pure point
    of being, 91; quasi-being, 113,
    114; radical Infinity of Being, 64;
    withdrawal of, xxii
Being and Event (Badiou), xviii, xxii,
    xxiii, xxvii, xxxii
benevolence, 125
the body, 21; of Christ, 135, 148; of
    Church, 141; of God, 135; the soul
    and, 42; thought and, 29
Bossuet, Jacques-Bénigne, 14, 16; Fénelon
    and, 48; funeral orations of, 47
bourgeois ideology, 150

calculating subject, 65
Calvinism, 60
Catholicism, 135
causality, 78, 115–16, 123; Christ and,
    76–77; divine action and, 22; God
    and, 39
Century, The (Badiou), xx
certainty, 35
Chants de Maldoror (Lautréamont), xiii
Châtelet, François, xiv
China, 12, 18, 36, 40
Christ, xxx, 144, 152, 168; as Architect
    of Eternal Temple, xxxi, 33, 127,
    142, 146, 147, 149; body of, 135, 148;
    causality and, 76–77; Christ the
    Son, 11; Church and, xxxvii, 134;
    coming of, 76; de-eventalization
    of, 76; desire of, 140, 146; end of,
    144; failure of, 145; the Fall and, 112;
    finite world and, 134; God and, 142,
    145–46; as God as unconscious, 153,
    159; grace, Christ cause of, 131; grace
    of, 51, 52; as Head of the Church,
    33, 36, 147, 148, 149; humiliation
    of, 89; marriage of, 167; meaning
    and, 12; Pascal and, xxix; plan of,
    139; polyvalence of, 127; prayer and,
    150; as quasi-nothingness, 99; as
    Redeemer, 26; as Repairer of the
    World, 26; the righteous and, 148;
    seduction of, 126; soul of, 139, 141;
    thought of, 158; time and, 143; total
    knowledge of, 154; two functions
    of, 33; universal import of, 31; as
    universal mediator, 125; work of,
    145, 147
Christianity, xxix, xxxvi, 19, 102;
    Cartesianism and, 38; categories of,
    30, 55; China and, 18; Chinese as
    unwitting Christians, 36; dialectical
    figures composed by, 28; existential,
    32; form of overt criticism of,
    2; God and, 56; institutional
    power of, 13; intellectual essence
    and, 60–61; Jesuit order and,
    38; of Malebranche, 27–28;
    mathematization of, 28, 32, 37;
    minimal allegiance to categories
    of, 13; modernity and, 175; modern
    philosophy and, 8; non-Christians,
    142; ontology of, 101, 106; Pascal
    and, 10; phenomenology of
    Christian subject, 10; philosophical
    radicalism of Malebranche and,
    31; philosophy involving Christian
    categories, 15; rationalism and, 9,
    32, 40, 62; signifying structure of,
    32; subject, Christian notion of,
    84; true Christian philosophy, 8;
    universality of, 37

Church, xxviii, xxx, xxxi, 110, 171, 176;
  body of, 141; Christ and, xxxvii, 134;
  Christ as Head of the Church, 33,
  36, 147, 148, 149; communist parties
  and, 152; desire and, 102; Fathers,
  137; God, Creation, Christ and, 11;
  God establishing, 56; mankind and,
  134; materiality of, 148; orthodoxy
  of, 31; recruitment to, 148; the
  righteous and, 149; sin and, 148;
  world as site of, 25
class struggle, 55
Cohen, Paul, xxxv
Collège international de philosophie,
  xiv
Collège universitaire de Reims, xii
colonialism, 18
communism, xxiv; communist parties,
  149, 152; communist philosophy, 8;
  Third International, 150
confessors, 37, 38
consistency, xxxi
courage, 175
creationist dogma, 58, 59
Creation of the world, 11, 31, 94, 106
creative action, 67, 69
creative gesture: law of order and, 71;
  perfection in, 69, 72
crime and punishment, dialectic of,
  140
crucifixion, 98

damnation, 162, 163
de Chardin, Pierre Teilhard, 4
deduction, 32–33
Deleuze, Gilles, xiv, xx
de Mairan, Dortous, 2
democracy, xxiv
Derrida, Jacques, xiv, xviii

Descartes, René, xxii, xxv, xxxvi,
  176; anti-Cartesianism, 10–11;
  Cartesian axiomatics, 11,
  21; Cartesian rupture, xxiii;
  Christianity and Cartesianism, 38;
  first post-Cartesian generation,
  1; Jansenists and Cartesianism,
  41, 43; Malebranche and, 4;
  Meditations, 2; Mesland and, 9;
  modern philosophy and, 8; Pascal
  and, 10; on physiology, 3; problems
  with Cartesianism, 20; The Search
  After Truth and, 40; seeing and, 20;
  Spinoza and, 39; Treatise on Man,
  2, 41
de Sévigné, Madame, 17, 22, 49
desire, xxxi, 81, 109, 125, 141; Baroque
  and, 142; of Christ, 140, 146; Church
  and, 102; of desire, 106; finite
  desire, indestructibility of, 161–62;
  forever-unsatisfied, 167; for God,
  163–64, 166, 167, 168; of God, 65,
  66, 74, 86, 103, 110–14, 126, 145, 159;
  God's desire to be God, 94–95,
  98, 105, 106; grace and, 134, 150; of
  human subject, 160, 161, 165; for
  Infinite, 173; invincibility of, 162,
  164–65, 169; Lacan and, 66; law and,
  66, 96, 103, 139; pleasure of, 169;
  self-sufficiency and, 101; structure
  of, 136; suspension of, 166, 167, 168;
  unconscious object of, 163, 164
Devil and the Good Lord, The (Sartre),
  156
Dialogue Between a Christian Philosopher
  and a Chinese Philosopher
  (Malebranche), 12, 17, 18
dictatorship of the masses, xvii
discontinuity, 10

disorder, 71
divine action, 92; causality and, 22;
    Creation of the world as, 94; effect
    of, 161; general nature of, 151; glory
    and, 93, 95; local connectedness
    of, 132; mathematization of, 43;
    rationality and, 48
divine fantasy, 103
divine freedom, 92
divine functions, 83
divine glorification, 78
divine infallibility, 138
divine infinity, 77
divine inscrutability, 42
divine interiority, 81
divine intervention, 22, 76; faith and,
    110; mathematical legality and, 43
divine knowledge, 158
divine legality, 139
divine subject, 155, 159
divine will, 60, 103; arbitrariness of, 59
divine wisdom, 31, 60, 71, 120
dualism, 42; functional, 34;
    heterogeneous nature of
    thought and extension and, 29;
    radicalization of, 21

earthly subjects, 159
eâtre de la Commune, xv
ecclesial thought, 36
École normale supérieure (ENS), xiv, xv
École polytechnique, xiv
Eden, 108
eighteenth century, 57; apologetic
    works in, 4; the Enlightenment and,
    19; philosophy of, 17
Elements of the Philosophy of Right
    (Hegel), 140
endless pursuit, 167

enlightenment, 158
the Enlightenment, 19
ENS. See École normale supérieure
L'essence de la politique (seminar), 195
eternal Temple, xxxi, 33, 127, 138, 142,
    146, 149
ethics, xxx
Ethics (Badiou), xxxi
Ethics (Spinoza), 2
L'être 1. Figure ontologique: Parménide
    (seminar), 195
L'être 2. Figure théologique: Malebranche
    (seminar), xxi, 195
L'être 3. Figure du retrait: Heidegger
    (seminar), 195
Eucharist, 9, 135
Euclidean space, 21
evil, 49, 68, 89; admiration of, 72;
    essence of, 69; God explicitly
    willing, 87; as non-being, 70;
    positive, 88; question of, 93
execution, 6
Experimental University of Vincennes,
    xiii
extremist thesis, 59; arguments
    directed against, 73; tragic, 63

fabrication, metaphor of, 67
faith, 30, 119; articles of, 56; divine
    intervention and, 110
the Fall, 26, 75, 76, 78, 91, 108; Christ
    and, 112; sin and, 120
Father and the Son, 28, 91, 105, 106
favor, 122
Fénelon, François, 14, 16; Bossuet and, 48
fidelity, xxx
finite world: Christ and, 134; finite
    desire, indestructibility of, 161–62;
    finite objects, 163; God and, 58;

Infinite and, 59, 63, 77, 103; as
mediation of Infinite, 64; nature
and, 63; nothingness and, 88
formalism, xviii
Foucault, Michel, xiv
freedom, 165
French Communist Party, xxvi

Galas, Didier, xv
Galilean revolution, xxvii
Galileo Galilei, 10, 61
Gaullist France, xii
general equilibrium, 72
general will, 48, 74, 116
Girard, René, 137
glory, 58, 102, 118, 137, 140; almost
nothing and, 64; divine action and,
93, 95; enigma of, 106; of God, 33,
57, 142; Infinite and, 88; Other and,
79; questions of, 89
God, xxix, xxxvi, 88, 151, 162; action
of, 21–22, 66; apparent weakness
of, 119; Baroque artist God, 83,
92; of the Bible, 11; body of, 135;
capacity for nothingness, 79;
causality and, 39; Christ and,
142, 145–46; Christ as God as
unconscious, 153, 159; Christianity
and, 56; Church established by, 56;
constant intervention of, 73; death
of, 32; desire for, 163–64, 166, 167,
168; desire of, 65, 66, 74, 86, 103,
110–14, 126, 145, 159; evil explicitly
willed by, 87; the Father, 11; finite
world and, 58; general good of, 163;
general will of, 48; glory of, 33, 57,
142; God's desire to be God, 94–95,
98, 105, 106; Incarnation and, 91;
inscrutability of, 49; Kant and,

74; law, God submission to, 104;
without law, 97; mankind, interest
in, 157; materiality of, 148; meaning
and, 95–96; nothingness as other-
than-God, 90; occasionalism and
vision in, 23; opportunistic thesis
and glory of, 58; other-than-God,
102; perfection of, 67, 86; proofs
of existence of, 35; in quasi-
nothingness, 78; sadism of, 174; as
subject, 105, 143; temporalization
of, 153, 154; transcendence of, 42,
65; unconscious knowledge of, 158;
vision in, 20, 21, 30; wisdom of, 65
grace, xxvii, 11–12, 31, 99–100;
aesthetics of, 84, 112; Arnauld and
Malebranche arguments over, 47;
cause of, 124–25; of Christ, 51, 52;
Christ cause of, 131; of Creator, 51,
52; desire and, 134, 150; dispensation
of, 114–19, 125, 129–30, 135, 139, 144,
171; distribution of, 70, 130–31, 168;
effect of, 135; of enlightenment, 54,
158; eternity-time relationship and,
127; of feeling, 54; global aspects
of, 53; human subject and, 168;
incompleteness of, 144; insufficient
amount of, 136; Jansenists and,
18, 51; law of, 51, 55, 121, 123; local
aspects of, 53; mathematics of, 43,
130; movements of, 147; nature and,
46; occasional cause of, 133, 140,
158; order of, 157; physics of, 116;
prayer and, 149; problem of, 146;
quasi-being and, 114; question of,
52; refusal of, 153; revolutionary,
55; salvation and, 42; seventeenth
century and, 113
Gueroult, Martial, xxxvi, 26

Hegel, Georg Wilhelm Friedrich, xxii, xxxvi, 95; *Elements of the Philosophy of Right*, 140; Hegelian dialectic, xiii, 8; Malebranche and, 64; subjectivity and, 65
hell, 114, 117
heresy, 15, 49
high-society, 17, 44, 49
Holland, 45, 46
human multiplicity, xxxi
human soul, 113
human subject, 162; desire of, 160, 161, 165; doctrine of, 155; grace and, 168; macroscopic nature of, 156; quasi-nothingness and, 157; spiritual order of, 157
humiliation, 88–89

ignorance, 68, 152
Images du temps présent: qu'est-ce que vivre? (seminar), 195
immanentism, 64
immediacy, 34
impoverished monumentality, 23
improvisation, xix
Incarnation, 75; God and, 91; tragedy of, 32
L'Infini. Aristote, Spinoza, Hegel (seminar), 195
Infinite: desire for, 173; finite as mediation of, 64; finite world and, 59, 63, 77, 103; glory and, 88; infinite beauty, xxx; infinite objects, 163; nothing and, 58; One and, xxiii, xxxvi; radical Infinity of Being, 64; solitary infinity, 106
intellectual aristocratism, 4
intelligibility: of Being, xxxvi; of nature, 55; principles of, 53

intercession, 136–37, 153
interpretation, 10
intersubjectivity, 134
invincibility, 162, 164–65, 169; non-invincibility, 170

Jansenists, 17; affair, 15; apologetics and, 60; Cartesianism and, 41, 43; grace and, 18, 51; Le Vassor and, 44; party, xxvi, 38; political authorities tensions with, 45
Jesuit order, xxvi, 1, 22; Christianity and, 38; colonialism and, 18; confessors of, 38; *Dialogue Between a Christian Philosopher and a Chinese Philosopher* and, 18; Jansenists and, 17; Malebranche and, 37–38; missionaries, 36; preachers of, 57; in seventeenth century, 18
jouissance, 122
Journal de Trévoux, 18
Jules Ferry auditorium, xvii
justice, 175

Kant, Immanuel, xxii, xxxvi, 73, 74
Kierkegaard, Søren, 176

Lacan, Jacques, xi, xiii, 98; desire and, 66; ENS and, xv; Maoism and, xxv; Milner on, xvii–xviii; on the real, 90
lack, 86
Lacoue-Labarthe, Philippe, xv
Lautréamont, Comte de, xiii
law, 23, 130; desire and, 66, 96, 103, 139; discovering, 50; general, 135, 157; God submission to, 104; God without, 97; of grace, 51, 55, 121, 123; of nature, 55, 115; non-law, 42; of order, 66, 67, 71; universal, 74

legalism, 24, 42, 43
Leibniz, Gottfried Wilhelm, xxiii,
   xxvii, xxxvi, xxxvii; diplomacy
   and, 5; Malebranche and, 4, 16, 38,
   82–83; Spinoza and, 5
Lenin, Vladimir, xxxii
Le Vassor, Michel, 44
libertines, 40, 62, 167
Librairie Arthème Fayard, xxi
local connectedness, 132
Logics of Worlds (Badiou), xviii
Louis XIV, 1, 40
luxuriant ornamentation, 23
Lyotard, Jean-François, xiv

Malebranche, Nicolas, xxi, xxii. *See also*
   specific topics
Malis, Marie-José, xv
Mallarmé, Stéphane, xiii
mankind, 112; Church and, 134; God
   interest in, 157; "perfect man," 143
Maoism, xxiv, xxv
Mao Zedong, 72
Maria Theresa, Queen, 47
Marx, Karl, 8
Marxism, 55
materialism, 40, 61, 62
mathematics: Christianity,
   mathematization of, 28, 32, 37;
   divine action, mathematization
   of, 43; divine intervention,
   mathematical legality and, 43;
   general project of mathematization,
   133; of grace, 43, 130; logico-
   mathematical formalism, xviii;
   nature, mathematization of, 41, 42
mathemes, 19, 54
matrical core, 20
meaning, 12, 35, 95–96

mediation, 64
Meditations (Descartes), 2
Meditations on Humility (Malebranche), 12
Mesland, Father, 9
metaphorical objects, 164, 172
Milner, Jean-Claude, xvii–xviii
miracles, 99
misers, xxx, 142, 144, 145, 147
missionaries, 36, 40
Mitterrand, François, xxiv
modernity, 9, 13, 175
modern philosophy: Christianity and,
   8; Descartes and, 8; theology and, 11
moral merit, 170
mothers, 6–8
multiplicity, xxxvi, 27, 68
mystical interiority, 48

nature: aesthetics of, 119; finite
   world and, 63; grace and, 46;
   intelligibility of, 55; law of, 55,
   115; mathematization of, 41, 42;
   natural action, 22, 57; order of, 157;
   simplicity of ways and, 118
New Testament, xxviii
Nietzsche, 20
non-analytical reason, 10
non-Christian philosophies, 40
nothingness, 77, 102; almost nothing,
   59, 64, 68; Being and, 89, 103,
   139, 140; evil as nothingness, 68;
   finite world and, 88; God capacity
   for, 79; impossible nature of, 90;
   Infinite and, 58; as other-than-
   God, 90; ugliness and, 84. *See also*
   quasi-nothingness

objectivity, 36, 83
object-world, 105

objet a, 112
obscurantism, 132, 137
obstacles, 10
occasionalism, 20, 21, 23
Old Testament, xxviii, 92, 112
One, philosophical category of, xxi,
    xxii, xxiii, xxxvi, 27
ontology: aesthetic, 70, 82, 115, 117,
    131, 176; articulations of, xxviii;
    Being, ontological figure of, xxii;
    of Christianity, 101, 106; history of,
    xxxvi; immanentist, 63; ontological
    legalism, 24, 42; political, xxviii,
    xxxii, xxxiii, 25; proliferation of
    being under ontological laws, 23;
    subjective, 65, 82; subtractive, 36;
    theology and, 63
On True and False Ideas (Arnauld), 46
opportunistic thesis, 58
oral presentation, xix
Oratorians, 1, 41; Malebranche
    criticized by leadership of, 49;
    primary reference of, 48
organization, theory of, 149, 151
orientation in life, xviii
orthodoxy, 15, 31
Other, 79, 86

Paris 8, xiii
parliamentarism, xxiv
Parmenides, xxiv, 23
particular goods, 165
particular will, 72, 73, 74
Pascal, Blaise, xxvi, xxvii, 27, 112, 174;
    apologetics and, 60; Being and,
    xxviii; Christ and, xxix; Christianity
    and, 10; Descartes and, 10; on
    history of truth, 25; Malebranche
    and, 13, 16, 175; opposition to, 53;

Scholastics and, 61; Spinoza and, 9;
    theory of subject and, xxxiii
peasant culture, 71
Pensées (Pascal), xxvii
perfection, 66, 83; aesthetic perfection,
    72; in creative gesture, 69, 72; of
    God, 67, 86; practical, 70; self-
    sufficiency and, 101; subjective, 70
Peter, xxix
*Philosophical and Theological Reflections
    on the New System of Nature and
    Grace* (Arnauld), 46
philosophical didactics, xxxv
philosophical radicalism of
    Malebranche, 29, 176; Christianity
    and, 31; compensation for, 30;
    moderation and, 34, 37; paradoxical
    nature of, 54
physical sciences, 8
physiology, 3
Pius (Saint), 7
Plato, xiii, xvi, xix, xxii, xxxvi; on evil,
    68; tripartition of soul, 164
Platon: La République (seminar), 195
pleasure, 169, 170
Pluche, Noël-Antoine (Abbé), 4, 57
political normalization, xiii, xvii
Political Organization, The, xxiv
Port-Royal, 17
Pour aujourd'hui: Platon! (seminar),
    195
practical universalism, 73, 74
prayer, 149, 150
preachers, 57, 170
prevenient delectation, 170, 172
Prince of Condé, 17
proliferation, 24
propaedeutic teaching, xii
psychoanalysis, 162

public opinion, xix
Pumpkins, The (Badiou), xv

quasi-nothingness, 77; Christ as, 99;
    God in, 78; human subject and, 157
Queen Mother, 6
Que signifie «changer le monde»?
    (seminar), 195
quietism, 48

rain metaphor, 70–71, 120
Rancière, Jacques, xiv
rationality, 132; Cartesian rationalism,
    28; Christianity, rationalism and,
    9, 32, 40, 62; divine action and, 48;
    faith and, 30; figures of, 3; modern
    rationalism, 62; rationalization,
    5; salvation, apparent injustice of
    and, 34; scientific rationalism, 62;
    theology, rational, 31
the real, 90
Redeemer, 26, 75, 87
Redemption, 11, 75
Refutation of Father Malebranche's System
    on Nature and Grace (Fénelon), 48
Regnault, François, xvii
Reims, xii
religion: adoration, religious, 64;
    categories of, 33; fundamental
    categories of, xxxvii, 11; mass
    subjectivity of, 33–34; mystical
    interiority in, 48; particularity,
    religious, 31; politico-religious
    conflict, 17; salvation and, 42;
    Spinoza and, 39
Repairer of the World, 26
repression, 163
resurrection, 143
Revelation, 107

Rêveries (Rousseau), 169
the righteous, 146, 147; Christ and, 148;
    Church and, 149
Rimbaud, Arthur, xiii
Rousseau, Jean-Jacques, 169

sadism, 174
Sainte-Beuve, Charles-Augustin, 14
Saint Paul: The Foundation of
    Universalism (Badiou), xx
salvation, 28, 33, 57, 119, 120; aesthetics
    of, 84; apparent injustice of, 34;
    grace and, 42; religion and, 42
Sartre, Jean-Paul, 156
Schiaretti, Christian, xv
Scholastics, 61
Schopenhauer, Arthur, xii
Scripture, 35, 107
Search After Truth, The (Malebranche),
    3, 4; Arnauld and, 18; Book 2 of,
    6; Descartes and, 40; theology
    and, 12
seeing, 20
self-externalization, 88, 90
self-sufficiency, 97, 101, 106
Séminaire. Lacan: l'antiphilosophie 3, Le,
    1994–95 (Badiou), xxii
seminars, xx, 195; form of, xvii;
    improvisation of, xix; meaning of,
    xi; publishing of, xiv; purpose of,
    xviii; size of, xvi
sensible things, 34
Serres, Michel, xiv
Seuil, xiii
seventeenth century, 13; grace and, 113;
    Jesuit order in, 18; philosophy of, 17
simplicity of ways, 72, 85; acting
    according to, 91; aesthetic law of,
    97; nature and, 118

sin, 110; abominable, 164; Church and, 148; the Fall and, 120; original, 75, 76; temptation and, 123
Socialist Party, xxiv
Socrates, xviii
Son as God, 78
S'orienter dans la pensée, s'orienter dans l'existence (seminar), 195
the soul, 42
Spectacle of Nature, The (Pluche), 4
Spinoza, Baruch, xxii, xxiii, xxxvi, 49, 90, 161; Descartes and, 39; Ethics, 2; Leibniz and, 5; Malebranche accused of Spinozism, 40; Malebranche and, 4, 16; modernity and, 13; Pascal and, 9; religion and, 39
spiritual abdication, xxxvii
Stalin, Joseph, xxxii, xxxiii, 149, 152
subjectivity, 33–34; categories of, 61; Christian notion of subject, 84; God as subject, 105, 143; Hegel and, 65; intersubjectivity, 134; subjective determination, 54; subjective ontology, 65, 82
subjectivo-dialectical filiation, 61
subject-object, 125
subtractive movements, 36
success of Malebranche, 14, 15; philosophical success, 16; worldly success, 17
superego, 175
Symposium (Plato), xix

temple metaphor, 70–71
temptation, 33, 123, 136, 147; exposure to, 151; succumbing to, 150
Théâtre de la Commune, xvii
theology, 13, 156; classical, 15; dispute of, 15; modern philosophy and, 11; ontology and, 63; rational theology,

31; The Search After Truth and, 12; substructure of, 136; theological mathemes, 19
Théorie axiomatique du Sujet (seminar), 195
Théorie du Mal, théorie de l'amour (seminar), 195
theory of subject, xxxii, xxxiii
Theory of the Subject (Badiou), xiii
Third International, xxv, xxxiii, 150
Thomism, 9, 106
thought and extension, 29
time, 126; Christ and, 143; end of, 144; God, temporalization of, 153, 154; grace, and eternity-time relationship and, 127
tragic thought, 61
Traité de la nature et de la grâce. See Treatise on Nature and Grace
transcendence, 42, 65; de-radicalizing, 81; unbearable, 62
transgressive capacity, 98, 99
Treatise on Man (Descartes), 2, 41
Treatise on Nature and Grace (Traité de la nature et de la grâce) (Malebranche), xxi, xxii, xxvii, 131; Arnauld and, 46; circumstances surrounding publication of, 41; Discourses of, 50, 108; editions of, 19, 50; influence of, 14; meaning of first sentence of, 25; non-Christian philosophy and, 40; "On Grace: On the Way It Acts in Us," 51; "On the Laws of Grace in Particular, and on the Occasional Causes Which Govern em and Which Determine their Efficacy," 51; "On the Necessity of the General Laws of Nature and Grace," 50, 54; publication of, 43, 47; Third Discourse of, 160

Treatise on the Love of God (Malebranche), 12

UCFML. *See* Union of Communists of France, Marxist-Leninist
ugliness, 84
uncertainty, 35
the unconscious, doctrine of, 159
L'Un. Descartes, Platon, Kant (seminar), 195
Union of Communists of France, Marxist-Leninist (UCFML), xxiv, xxv
universality, 37
universal wills, 73
University of Nancy, xii

Vérité et Sujet (seminar), 195

virtual capacity, 152
virtue, xxix
virtuosity, of Malebranche, 87
Voltaire, 62
Vrin publishing house, 19

Wahl, François, xiii
wisdom, 109
Wittgenstein's Antiphilosophy (Badiou), xx
women, 167
workman, metaphor of, 67

Le xxe siècle (seminar), 195

Yves André (father), 18

Žižek, Slavoj, xviii

List of the seminars
(in chronological order)

1983–1984	L'Un. Descartes, Platon, Kant.
1984–1985	L'Infini. Aristote, Spinoza, Hegel.
1985, 4e trim.	L'être 1. Figure ontologique: Parménide.
1986, 1er trim.	L'être 2. Figure théologique: Malebranche.
1986–1987	L'être 3. Figure du retrait: Heidegger.
1987–1988	Vérité et Sujet.
1988–1989	Beckett et Mallarmé.
1989–1990	Platon: La République.
1990–1991	Théorie du Mal, théorie de l'amour.
1991–1992	L'essence de la politique.
1992–1993	L'antiphilosophie 1. Nietzsche.
1993–1994	L'antiphilosophie 2. Wittgenstein.
1994–1995	L'antiphilosophie 3. Lacan.
1995–1996	L'antiphilosophie 4. Saint Paul.
1996–1998	Théorie axiomatique du Sujet.
1998–2001	Le xxe siècle.
2001–2004	Images du temps présent: qu'est-ce que vivre?
2004–2007	S'orienter dans la pensée, s'orienter dans l'existence.
2007–2010	Pour aujourd'hui: Platon!
2010–2012	Que signifie «changer le monde»?